COLLECTOR'S GUIDES

Glock

THE WORLD'S HANDGUN

D1607268

COLLECTOR'S GUIDES
Glock
THE WORLD'S HANDGUN

Chris McNab

amber
BOOKS

Copyright © 2015 Amber Books Ltd

All rights reserved. No part of this publication may be reproduced, stored in a retrieval system, or transmitted in any form or by any means, electronic, mechanical, photocopying, recording, or otherwise, without prior written permission of the copyright holder.

Published by
Amber Books Ltd
74–77 White Lion Street
London
N1 9PF
United Kingdom
www.amberbooks.co.uk
Appstore: itunes.com/apps/amberbooksltd
Facebook: www.facebook.com/amberbooks
Twitter: @amberbooks

ISBN 978-1-78274-256-2

Project Editor: Michael Spilling
Design: Zoë Mellors
Picture Research: Terry Forshaw

Printed in China

Contents

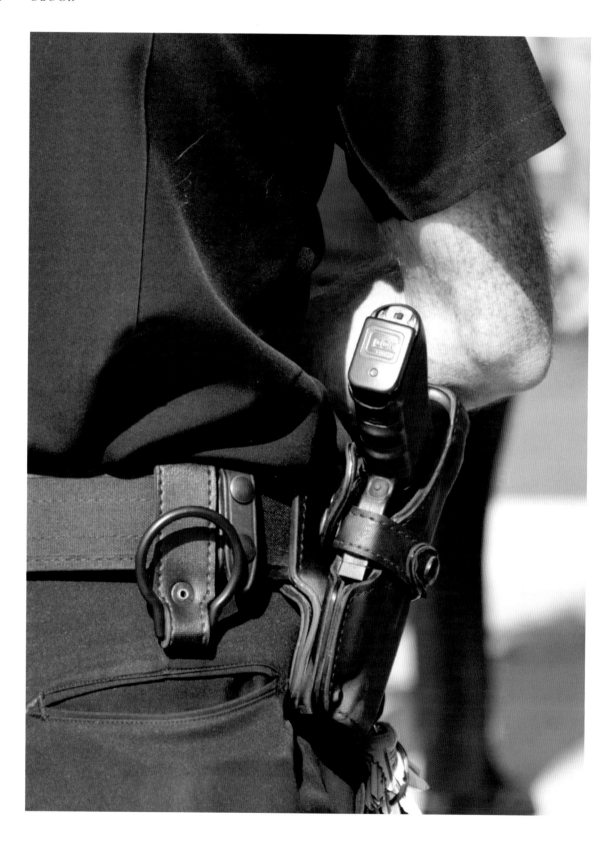

Introduction

How does a gun become iconic? Don't immediately think that this is to do with the level of quality exhibited by the weapon. Firearms history is littered with excellent pieces of kit that are scarcely known to anyone outside the specialist firearms fraternity. How many members of the general public would be able to identify, say, a Sig P220 or a Steyr M handgun, both excellent weapons? Nor is iconicity necessarily dependent on some seminal advance in firepower. Kalashnikov's AK, undoubtedly the world's most famous rifle, doesn't actually offer superior firepower characteristics compared to many other fully automatic assault rifles.

I would argue that three characteristics have to combine to give a firearm an iconic status—usability, reliability, and visibility. The first characteristic, usability, refers to the ease with which the weapon can be loaded, fired, stripped, cleaned, and generally maintained. Any weapon that is awkward to handle, and doesn't feel good in the hand, will quickly fall from favor and from the market. Reliability is one aspect of that usability. We must always remember that many firearms, including the Glock, are intended for law enforcement or military use. For soldiers and police officers, a jammed gun can literally mean the difference between life and death in a deadly-force encounter. So, a successful firearm is one that will send out rounds consistently and on target without failure, even after many years or even decades of use.

Usability and reliability are very understandable concepts, even for the layman. But what exactly do I mean by visibility? Visibility refers to both the scale of distribution

FACING PAGE: A US police officer wears his Glock handgun—the Glock has almost become the defining pistol of American law enforcement.

BELOW: Gaston Glock revolutionized the principles of handgun design with the eponymous Glock, despite having no prior experience of firearms production.

of the weapon and the extent to which the product's qualities are understood and appreciated. Take the AK rifle, for example. Who would deny that one of the central pillars underpinning its notoriety is the fact that it is the most mass-produced and widely distributed weapon in history (if we take the entire Kalashnikov series)? From entire armies to small insurgent groups and individual criminals, AKs have, in a sense, literally armed the post-war world, and have thus achieved the media presence that makes that curved 30-round magazine a globally familiar profile.

BELOW: Austrian police officers wear their Glocks in quick-draw holsters, also made from the tough Glock polymer.

Modern Icon

This book is focused squarely on the Glock series of handguns, which for reasons that will become progressively apparent, has also achieved something of an iconic status. Which is curious, because generally speaking handguns don't have the same pull on the public imagination as rifles, submachine guns, and machine guns. There are some exceptions—James Bond has given international prestige to the Walther PPK, although apart from being compact the PPK actually has little to recommend it as a combat handgun. Another Hollywood darling is the .44 Magnum Smith & Wesson (S&W) Model 29, popularized by Clint Eastwood in his husky portrayal of Harry Callaghan in the *Dirty Harry* series of movies. The Colt M1911, by contrast, has earned its stripes through more laudable means— longevity, wide distribution (and copying), and the thumping power of the .45 ACP cartridge.

That an Austrian handgun, developed for the Austrian Army by a man with no previous experience of firearms design, in 9mm caliber (not an especially powerful round) should enter this select pantheon is curious. What Gaston Glock brought to the world was a revolution in design. In every aspect of its construction, material technology and functionality, the Glock was a game-changer. Widely referred to as the "plastic pistol" (not always affectionately), on account of the substantial use of polymer materials in its construction, the Glock 17 handgun entered the market in 1983, offering a light, sleek, quick-firing 9mm (0.354in) handgun with a 17-round magazine capacity. These qualities not only endeared it to the Austrian Army, but also to military units and law-enforcement agencies throughout the world, plus hundreds of thousands of civilian shooters looking for a good personal protection or sporting handgun.

The World's Handgun

Glock handguns are today used in official capacities in more than 50 countries around the world, with private sales going to many more. What really catapulted the Glock to public prominence, however, was its widespread adoption by the US police forces and law-enforcement agencies. Today, around 70 percent of the United States' 900,000 police officers have Glocks on their hips, an astonishing achievement considering that each of the country's police departments typically has autonomous choice over their handgun acquisition. The high percentage of police issue also means that the public at large has become familiar with the Glock profile, and this awareness has been expanded by Hollywood and TV. Some of the dozens of movie stars who have wielded the Glock on the big screen include Bruce Willis, Tommy Lee Jones, Mickey Rourke, and Robert Downey Jr. Nor is this cinematic acquisition entirely accidental. The Glock company has been judiciously active in providing film companies with access to its weaponry through authorized suppliers, giving the handgun what Glock historian Paul Barrett has called its "*Dirty Harry* moment."

But apart from the hype, the Glock series of handguns are fine weapons—their popularity has a sound basis in technology and performance. This book will delve into Glock handguns both in terms of design and functionality. What we will see is a weapon created for the hard realities of use, by people whose lives have to depend on 1.56 pound (0.71 kg) of plastic and metal strapped to their hips. Although this story is not without its controversies, the vast majority of those people have not been disappointed.

Development of the Glock

To understand the Glock, you need to comprehend the market that it entered in the 1980s, and something about the products against which it competed. The key categories of handgun had been settled during the first decade of the twentieth century, and by the post-war years there had been little seminal advance in the basic technology.

FACING PAGE: Officers of the Royal Canadian Mounted Police (RCMP) line up with their Glocks alongside Alaskan State Troopers (AST) during a shooting competition.

Handguns fell into two types—revolvers and semi-automatic pistols. The revolvers were the old guard, with an ancestry dating back to the days of the Wild West. In military use, revolvers had largely been replaced by pistols, but up until the Glock era the same could not be said for law-enforcement service. In the United States, for example, six-shot .38, .357 Magnum and (less commonly) .44 handguns were dominant among police forces until the 1980s and 1990s. Classic examples were the Colt Detective Special, the Ruger Speed-Six and the Smith & Wesson Model 10.

As with all types of firearms, revolvers had their pluses and minuses. One of the great virtues of the revolver was its reliability. Revolvers would rarely ever jam, and if there was a misfire all the operator typically had to do is simply pull the trigger once again to turn to the next cartridge; with a pistol, the user has to clear the jam manually, and sometimes empty and reload the gun. Unless the revolver's hammer was cocked, the gun also had the mechanical advantage that no parts (such as a firing pin) are held under spring tension, thereby reducing the possibility of mechanical wear. There were also some bonuses in ergonomics, particularly considering the fact that within a police force one gun would have to be used by a variety of human hand sizes. Because revolvers don't need to hold a magazine in the stock, they can be used more easily by individuals with small or slender hands.

So far, so good, but revolvers had a major deficit—ammunition capacity. The maximum number of cartridges they could hold was six, and six rounds could be burned through with frightening speed during an actual armed engagement. Speed-loading devices were developed, in which new rounds could be dropped into the empty chambers in one go, once the spent cases had been ejected, but revolvers still required frequent reloading, and in these moments the user was exposed and vulnerable.

The striking virtue of pistols, by contrast, was that they could offer greater ammunition capacity, and that meant greater firepower and less downtime between shooting. Instead of the rotating cylinder of the revolver, they had a detachable magazine inserted (usually) into the pistol grip—reloading was a simply matter of pressing the magazine eject button, then inserting a new magazine into the grip. The weapon then used the forces generated by firing—usually in either a blowback or recoil mechanism—to work through the cycle of extraction, ejection, and reloading.

BELOW: Handloading a revolver chamber by chamber is a slow business compared to the rapid mag reload of a semi-auto handgun.

First Automatics

The first automatic handguns had been developed at the end of the 19th century, and by World War I they had achieved acceptance. Some landmark weapons had been developed by 1914. In the United States, the Colt M1911 had set a design that was so successful it is still replicated and copied to this day. A short-recoil weapon firing a powerful .45 ACP cartridge, the M1911 used a swinging-link system to facilitate the locking action between barrel and slide. When the slide was forward, and a round chambered, lugs on the top of the barrel locked into corresponding grooves in the slide wall. When the gun was fired, the blowback forces drove the slide and barrel back together until the swinging link mechanism, attached to the rear of the barrel, pulled the barrel down and the lugs/grooves disengaged, allowing the slide to run through its complete recoil cycle and reload the gun.

The M1911 was undoubtedly the landmark US handgun of the twentieth century, one that would be the standard US Army issue pistol from 1911 until its replacement by the Beretta 92 in 1985. In Europe, pistol design took some different directions. The Soviets produced short-recoil workhorse handguns such as the 7.62 x 25mm Tokarev TT30, based heavily on the Colt system of operation, or 9mm weapons like the Makarov and Stechkin. But

ABOVE: US soldiers conduct building-clearance training with their Beretta M9 handguns. The Beretta M9 has been the main handgun of the US military since 1985.

ABOVE: **A West German trainee fires a 9mm Walther P1 during training in the 1980s; the P1 was a post-war version of the Walther P38.**

some of the greatest advances in handgun design took place in Western Europe. In Germany, for example, the two defining handguns of the world war era were the Luger Parabellum P-08 and its eventual replacement, the Walther P-38. Both were 9mm (0.354in) weapons, but while the Luger worked on a toggle-lock mechanism, the P38 used a wedge-shaped locking plate to secure barrel and slide together at the moment of firing. (Although the 9mm Parabellum that both weapons fired was perfectly suited to straightforward blowback operation, at this moment in history the German authorities did not trust a handgun that didn't have positive locking, hence opted for short-recoil weapons.)

The P38 was an enduring success—it was the standard Bundeswehr firearm until 1994 (as the P1), served with dozens of other armies and police forces, and remains a popular civilian weapon to this day. Nor was it the only pistol in the Walther range. Pre-1945 weapons included the Walther PP series, which included James Bond's infamous PPK, and some diminutive blowback models such as the six-round .25 ACP Model 9. But there were alternative stirrings in Belgium, courtesy of the liaison between famous US gun designer John Browning and the Belgian gunmaker Fabrique Nationale de Herstal (FN). This liaison had begun in the early 20th century with the FN Browning M1900, a 7.65 x 17mm (.32 ACP) blowback handgun, but culminated in the 9mm Browning GP35 Hi-Power, which Browning began to design but which was completed after his death by FN designer Dieudonné Saive. Despite the "High Power" title, derived from the French *Grand Puissance*, the GP35 was actually no more powerful than any other 9mm handgun. However, it did break the mold in several important regards, and set a pattern that would have a direct influence on the future of gun design, including the Glock. Browning based the action on that of the Colt

M1911, although made some modifications to the trigger mechanism, and used a shaped cam mechanism instead of a swinging link control the slide and barrel engagement. What was really ground-breaking about the P35, however, was its 13-round magazine capacity, courtesy of a double-stack magazine. The GP35 might not have had the physical punch of an M1911, but it had nearly double the ammunition, and that could give a soldier a crucial advantage in a close-quarters firefight.

The GP35 went into production in 1935, and did well from the outset—35,000 guns were made before 1939, and during the war it was put into production by Canada (for Canadian and Chinese forces) and also by Germany after its occupation of Belgium in 1940. But this was nothing compared to the success of the GP35 after the war, once FN had reestablished indigenous control over the production. Reliable, fast-shooting,

BELOW: The Browning Hi-Power ushered in the age of high-capacity handguns, with its 13-round detachable box magazine.

and offering a then-unrivalled magazine capacity, the GP35 appealed to a post-war generation of armies wanting to upgrade personal firepower. The pistol was therefore adopted by the British Army in 1954 as the standard replacement for the .38 Enfield/Webley revolvers, and it served in this capacity until 2013, when it was chosen for replacement by the Glock 17 (more about this later). Some 55 other countries took it on board in various official roles, and it remains in prolific use.

New Types

During the 1950s to 1970s, the European manufacturers especially began to roll out numerous new pistols, with more attention to the ergonomics of gun design and improvements in production quality. Companies like Steyr (Austria), Sig-Sauer (Switzerland), Heckler & Koch (Germany), Beretta (Italy), Star (Spain) and çeská zbrojovka Uherský Brod (CZUB) (Czechoslovakia) produced dozens of new models between them, advancing the type in terms of design, ergonomics, and safety. In Germany, for example, Heckler & Koch introduced the HK4 in 1967, a gun that looked back toward the Mauser HSc in terms of overall design, but which had interchangeable barrels so that caliber could be changed between 9mm Short (.380 ACP), 7.65mm (.32 ACP), 6.35mm (.25 ACP) and .22 LR (5.56mm). It was a double-action to single action pistol, meaning that the trigger pull alone cocked and released the hammer for the first shot, and the subsequent blowback action of the slide cocked the hammer for subsequent shots.

H&K subsequently upped its game with guns such as the double-action roller-delayed blowback P9S and the P7 (1976), the latter featuring a squeeze-action cocking handle integral with the pistol grip. SiG-Sauer, meanwhile, produced two landmark weapons—the P220 (1974) and the P225 (1978). The P220, for example, came in numerous calibers—9mm Para, 7.65mm Para, .38 Super, .45 ACP and .22 LR (the latter in the training variant of the gun). With an eye to the military and police markets, both of which demanded exacting safety requirements, the P220 had a four-point safety system, consisting of a decocking lever (set on the left side of the grip), patented firing pin safety block, a safety intercept notch, and trigger bar disconnector. It was a high-quality and persuasive weapon, and became the standard-issue sidearm of the Swiss Army. The P225 was, in effect, a shortened version of the P220.

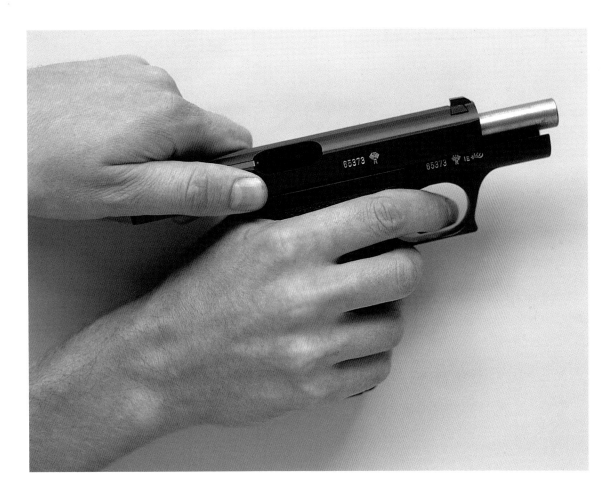

ABOVE: An operator draws back the slide on a Heckler & Koch P7 handgun. The P7 uses a distinctive gas-delayed blowback operating system.

Nor were the US manufacturers idle. As well as facing the influx of European models, the M1911 was joined by an increasing number of indigenous products, particularly from the 1950s onward. Colt's age-old rival, Smith & Wesson, came out with its first generation of semi-auto handgun in the form of the Model 39 of 1954, chambered for either 9mm Luger or .40 S&W. This weapon held eight rounds in a single-column magazine stack, but in the subsequent 9mm Parabellum Model 59, produced from 1971, this capacity jumped to 14 rounds, the significant advance in capacity due to a double-stack magazine. The M1911, by contrast, held just seven rounds.

Yet although the firearms differed between caliber types, layouts, and even operating principles, there was much uniting them. For a start, most of the guns were made of high-quality machining processes, which demanded extensive production lines and numerous well-trained engineering staff. The days of computer-numerical-control (CNC) machines, with their capability

ABOVE: A Czech CZ 75 handgun (here apparently having some ejection issues). The CZ 75 has been a global export success story.

to deliver multiple manufacturing processes in a single unitary process, had yet to embed themselves in industry. Furthermore, guns tended to still rely on high-quality steel and wood for their build (although pistol grip plates tended to be plastic, however). In short, they were expensive.

For this reason, it was often cheaper for large law enforcement bodies, such as the US police forces, to purchase relatively cheap revolvers rather than costly precision-engineered pistols from the European or US manufacturers. At a tactical level, furthermore, it is notable that many of the pistols produced during the 1960s and 1970s scarcely offered a significant ammunition-capacity advantage anyway. The P220, for example, had six to eight rounds, depending on the barrel and the series variant. The HK4 held seven or eight rounds, while most of the Berettas of these decades had eight to 10 rounds. The Czechs did nod more toward the Browning Hi-Power with weapons like the globally successful CZ 75, with a double-stack magazine holding a prodigious 16 rounds. Generally, however, the large-capacity models were the exception.

Glock Enters the Market

This was the context into which a certain Gaston Glock pitched himself
in the early 1980s. What is incredible about his story, however, is the sheer
audacity of a man who, with absolutely no experience of gun manufacturing,
set about creating, manufacturing, and selling one the greatest handguns of
modern history.

Up until 1963, Gaston Glock's life bore little evidence of his future as a
giant of firearms manufacturing. Born on July 19, 1929, in Vienna, Austria,
Gaston Glock was the son of the railway worker, but he took the step into
engineering in his early adult years. His work, however, was in the distinctly
unglamorous world of radiator manufacturing, in which he rose to become
a plant manager. Yet the young Gaston was ambitious for his own business,
which he founded in 1963 with his wife, Helga.

At first, the Glock company focused
on commercial mundanities such as
doorknobs, curtain rods, and assorted
metal window fittings. The business was
built up in a very modest workshop,
but despite the limited production
capacity Glock took the work forward
successfully. He managed to secure
contacts within the Austrian Ministry of
Defense, and eventually began supplying
the Austrian Army with various
military products, principally knives and
bayonets, grenades, entrenching tools,
and machine-gun belts. Nothing, as yet,
spoke of firearms design. Glock hadn't
even much experience of using firearms,
apart from a very brief spell serving in
the German armed forces at the end of
World War II.

In February 1980, Glock was fortunate
enough to overhear a conversation
between two Austrian military
officers, discussing the fact that the
Austrian armed service was looking

**BELOW: A US patent
document reveals, in an
exploded diagrammatic
form, the operating system
of the Glock handgun,
showing the frame, slide,
and barrel groups.**

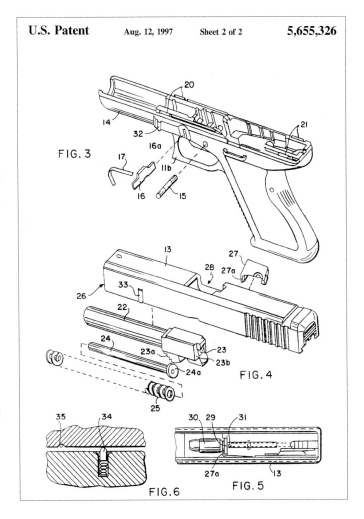

AUSTRIAN MINISTRY OF DEFENSE
HANDGUN SELECTION CRITERIA, 1980

1. The system has to be a self-loading pistol.

2. The pistol has to fire the 9mm S-round/P-08 (parabellum).

3. The magazine must be able to be filled without any auxiliary devices.

4. The magazine must have a minimum capacity of eight rounds.

5. All operations for:

    - preparation for firing

    - firing itself and

    - manipulation of the pistol after firing must be capable of being performed single-handed, right-handed as well as left-handed according to the choice of the user.

6. The technical safety of the pistol has to be absolutely guaranteed under any circumstances from:

    - shock

    - stroke [glancing impact]

    - dropping from a height of 2m (6.6ft) on a steel plate.

7. The main parts of the pistol should be dismantled for cleaning and reassembling without any tools.

8. Maintenance and cleaning of the pistol should be performed without the need for tools.

9. The components of the pistol must not exceed more than 58 parts (equivalent to the P-38).

10. Gauges, measuring, and testing devices must not be necessary for long-term maintenance.

11. The manufacturer must provide the Armed Force, at least at the point the pistol series is supplied, a complete set of drawings and exploded views. The drawings have to show measurements, tolerances, the materials used, surface treatment, and any other important details for the production of the pistol.

12. All the component parts must be interchangeable [between the pistols] without any modification.

13. During the firing of the first 10,000 rounds (using ammunition in accordance with valid TL regulations) no more than 20 jams are allowed, even if the jams do not require tools to clear them.

14. All the main parts of the gun will be examined and must be securely in place after the handgun has fired 15,000 rounds. Then the pistol will be tested with a test cartridge generating 5,000 bar pressure, after which the gun's main parts must continue to function properly and meet all the required technical specifications. If the gun cannot meet these requirements, then its testing cannot continue.

15. During correct use of the pistol the user must not be endangered in any way by the ejection of spent cartridge cases.

16. The muzzle energy must be at least 441.5 joules when firing a 9mm S-round/P-08 Hirtenberger Patronen AG.

17. Pistols that deliver less than 70 percent of the maximum points will not be issued for military use.

to replace the venerable Walther P38 as the standard pistol. Quickly, Glock moved in to find out more, despite the fact that he would be pitted against some of Europe's most experienced and august gunmakers. He inquired about the replacement, and was given the Ministry of Defense's (MoD) official procurement criteria. This constituted a list of 17 major points (see opposite), a truly demanding set of criteria with extremely high standards of reliability, maintainability, and user-friendliness, and showing a clear progressive evolution beyond the standards of the P38. Much to the incredulity of many, Glock decided to enter the race, which would be contested by companies with hundreds of years' combined experience. Nevertheless, Glock received approval from the MoD to enter the competition, and he set to work.

Development Stage

The first step for Glock in this Herculean challenge was to familiarize himself with modern handgun design. He purchased numerous weapons, which he stripped down and studied intently, getting to grips with the fundamental operating principles. But he wasn't going to rely entirely on his own self-tuition. In May 1980, he also gathered together a group of internationally respected firearms experts to consult them about what they wanted from the next generation of handguns. This consultation brought some judicious feedback. Reliability was obviously of key importance, asserted the experts. The gun needed to be light and slender in profile—meaning it was easy to slip into a holster—and it also had to have "pointability," meaning that the user could bring it to the point of aim almost instinctively. The experts also advocated that the MoD's stipulated maximum of 58 component parts for the handgun was too high, and recommended 40 instead. Keeping the number of parts low would ease maintenance and improve serviceability, as well as deliver obvious efficiencies for production.

One especially interesting discussion related to handgun safety. Most pistols at this time had a simple manually operated safety switch lever with "safe" and "fire" positions. The operator would, typically, engage the "safe" position when the gun was holstered, and then click it off to "fire" when the pistol was drawn with intent. However, in reality, and especially in the heat of tense or violent situations, users often forgot whether they had engaged the safety or not. This could result in either dangerous accidental discharges or, conversely, the weapon not firing at a moment when the user

GLOCK 17

DATE:
1982
CALIBER:
9 x 19mm
LENGTH:
8.03in (204mm)
BARREL LENGTH:
4.48in (114mm)
WEIGHT (LOADED):
32.12oz (910g)
MAGAZINE CAPACITY (STANDARD):
17
RANGE
50yds (45.72m)

really needed to send out rounds. Glock was particularly fascinated by this discussion, and set out to revise the principles of pistol safety.

Armed with the feedback from his expert panel, Gaston Glock, aided by his wife, Helga, and a small group of engineers and technicians, set out to produce a prototype gun that could be submitted to the MoD pistol competition. Note that he was still running his regular engineering business at this time, and much of the development took place in a basic workshop in the garage next to his house in Deutsch-Wagram. Despite his lack of experience, which to outsiders appeared profound, on April 30, 1981, Glock filed for a patent on a new weapon, known as the Glock 17. The following year on May 19, 1982, after a huge amount of additional investment in time and money, Glock submitted the Glock 17 to the military trials. He was about to make history.

Glock 17

It is now time to divert a little from the story of Glock's commercial adventure, and look more closely at his first gun. It took one glance at the gun to tell the informed firearms enthusiast that here was something different. In some ways, and speaking in the broadest of terms, the Glock was familiar. It was a short-recoil slide-operated handgun feeding from a detachable box magazine inserted into the stock. It also fired the ubiquitous 9mm Parabellum cartridge.

Yet look closer, and a world of divergences from conventional thinking begin to make themselves apparent. First, there was the matter of construction. Although the Austrian Army specifications had stipulated that the new handgun could not exceed 58 parts, the Glock dropped substantially below that limit. Depending slightly on how you count the parts, the Glock 17 had just 34 components. But one of the Glock advantages was that all these parts were completely interchangeable with those from any other Glock. Author Peter Alan Kasler, in his recommended 1992 book *Glock: The New Wave in Combat Handguns*, explains one exceptional demonstration of this quality:

ABOVE: **A rear view of two Glock magazines, showing how the viewing ports at the back reveal how many cartridges are loaded.**

"In May 1990, at the Raahaugee shooting Sports Fair in Ontario, California, members of the California Rangemasters Association fired 10,140 round of Federal 9mm Parabellum ammunition in a rather unique Glock pistol.

Twenty Glock Model 17s were completely disassembled. All their parts were then mixed up so it was impossible to determine which parts had been together in which pistols originally. Someone grabbed a receiver, serial number MU421US, and then all the other parts necessary to assemble one complete Model 17 were taken at random from the various piles.

Following assembly and function checks, magazines were loaded, and the firing began. Three hours and forty minutes later, 10,140 rounds had been fired. During that period the pistol was fieldstripped and the breechface and chamber were cleaned every 2,500 rounds. Also during the three hours and forty-seven minutes, mandatory cease-fires (remember, the testers were all range masters) for target changes were accomplished.

The pistol malfunctioned once: at 4,500 rounds a trigger spring ($1.95) broke. Another was grabbed from the mixed-up parts pile and installed in less than one minute, and firing resumed."

—Kasler (1992): pp. 132–33

Parts and Construction

This extraordinary feat demonstrated the perfect interchangeable of parts on the Glock. Although all handgun parts are machined to common measurements and specified tolerances, the individual tooling of the parts can mean that component replacement might require some work by a gunsmith before everything operates smoothly. By investing in the total uniformity provided by CNC computer-controlled machining, Glock developed what was in effect a collection of absolutely uniform parts, all of which could be assembled into an individual gun.

Such was very appealing to those who wanted convenient on-site maintenance of their handguns. Furthermore, as we shall see in the following chapter, the components of the Glock are grouped together logically in sections that, in many cases, can be dissembled, assembled, and modified without the use of tools.

RIGHT: This exploded view reveals the essential simplicity of the Glock 17, with just 34 components. Some rival handguns have nearly twice the number of parts.

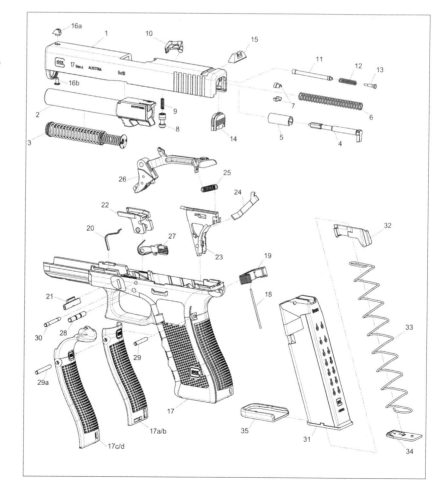

Another aspect of the Glock that stood out was the actual materials used in its construction. Glocks are often widely—and on occasions negatively—referred to as "plastic pistols." Two points arise. First, we must not get the impression that the Glock is almost entirely cast in plastic; in terms of weight the gun is still 83 percent steel. Also, "plastic" doesn't do justice to the capabilities of the actual polymer material used. The "Polymer 2," developed by Glock himself, is a non-fiberglass reinforced material that is even stronger than carbon steel despite being much lighter, and is hugely resistant to physical distortions from extreme temperatures. The actual test parameters for Glock pistols are +140°F (+60°C) down to -40°F (-40°C), but the Polymer 2 materials can actually exceed these limits by a significant degree.

So which parts are actually made from the polymer? These include the receiver (frame, although the slide rails are metal), recoil-spring guide rod, magazine catch, trigger and trigger housing, and even the magazine. What this meant in practical terms was a gun that was very light—the entire weapon weighed just 1.45 pounds (0.66kg), whereas many other handguns weighed more around the 1.98 pounds (0.9kg) mark—but which was also tough and hard wearing. But the Glock paid equal attention to the metal parts. Chief of these was the slide, which was machined directly out of bar

BELOW: A Glock 17 disassembled as it would be for a basic clean. Apart from some minor parts, nearly all of the lower receiver is made from polymer materials.

RIGHT: The Glock's low, flat profile makes it ideal for holstered use, while its absence of external safety switch means it can be drawn and fired rapidly.

stock to produce an extremely solid piece, with a visually distinct rectangular cross section. The other major metal component was the 4.48in (114mm) barrel. One point to note about the barrel, apart from its hexagonal rifling, is the fact that it is made to slightly tighter dimensions than many other 9mm (0.354in) pistols, equating to .356 (9.04mm) caliber. The grip this gives on the bullet means that there is a better gas seal between the bullet and bore, thus producing higher muzzle velocities than many other competing pistols.

Before moving on to the Glock's actual operating mechanism, another material element that needs mentioning is the Tenifer coating applied to many of the steel components, including the barrel bore and exterior of the slide. Tenifer is a trademark name for a case-hardening process, in which nitrogen and carbon are diffused into non-ferrous metals. What this means, in practical terms, is that the key metal parts of the Glock have mighty resistance to scratch and abrasion damage and to corrosion. The coating is actually impregnated into the metal to give it a skin hardness beyond that of metal alone, and the corrosion resistance exceeds many other protective coatings or materials, such as chrome plating, bluing, stainless steel, or Teflon.

Operating Mechanism

It is when we venture internally that we truly reveal the ground-breaking nature of the Glock. For a start, we have to acknowledge the Glock 17's standard magazine capacity of 17 rounds, an extraordinary figure, especially when compared to the six-shot revolvers with which many police officers around the world were struggling. The capacity is achieved by using a double-stack arrangement, and although it forms a chunky grip, the large number of rounds between reloads is appreciated by many.

As noted, the Glock was a short-recoil weapon, meaning that the force of recoil provided the motive power for the extraction and ejection cycle. (Short-recoil means that the barrel and slide recoil locked together for a distance less than the length of the cartridge case before the two disengage and the slide continues rearward. In long-recoil weapons, mainly heavy machine guns, the barrel and bolt recoil for more than the length of the case before unlocking.) The key innovations with the Glock's recoil mechanism lay in the method of locking the slide and barrel together for firing, and in the mechanism of disconnecting them during the recoil phase.

Compare the Glock to the M1911. As described earlier, the Colt's barrel locks into the slide via two lugs atop the barrel that engage with corresponding slide grooves. This interconnection holds the two components together as they recoil backward when the gun is fire, before the swinging link drops the rear of the barrel down (when the bullet has left the gun and the pressures have dropped to safe levels) and allows the slide to go backward through its cycle. The Glock, by contrast, locked the barrel and slide together by means of the rear of the barrel, formed into a rectangular block, dropping into and locking against the shoulders of the ejection port. This is an ingeniously simple action, and a robust one as well.

Beneath the barrel are two angled lugs. The rear lug serves as the feed ramp for the cartridges, guiding fresh rounds smoothly into the chamber ready for firing. The front lug serves as both an assistance to locking the gun firmly into battery, through engagement with a slide lock piece, but it also provides the means of disconnecting the barrel from the slide during recoil. When the gun is fired, the barrel and slide travel rearward under the force of recoil for a distance of about 0.06 inches (1.58mm).

At this point, the front lug then comes into contact with an angled and upward pointing piece of the locking block. As the two angled surfaces come together, the barrel is cammed downward and therefore disengages with the

ABOVE: An Iraqi army instructor fires a G17 pistol during training at the Police Training Academy at Camp India, Baghdad, Iraq.

slide. As the slide continues its way to the rear, against the pressure of the return spring, the spent cartridge case is extracted and ejected through the now-open ejection port. Then the slide returns forward to battery, stripping a fresh round from the top of the magazine to chamber it; the front barrel lug reengages with the locking-block piece, but this time the barrel is cammed upward to lock again for firing.

Firing Mechanism

The Glock mechanism was solid and dependable. But it was only a single aspect of an ingenious design. One thing that immediately struck those who first picked up the Glock was the absence of a hammer. In many handguns, such as the Colt M1911 and Browning Hi-Power, there is a hammer at the rear of the gun, which is cocked either by the user when he first pulls back the slide to chamber a cartridge, or by action of pulling the trigger (in double-action weapons) or by the recoil action of the slide when the gun is fired. The hammer is held in the cocked position under spring tension by a sear connected to the trigger; pull the trigger, and the sear moves and releases the hammer, which then drives forward to strike the firing pin and fire the cartridge.

The Glock, by contrast, has no hammer at all. Instead it has a spring-loaded firing pin, activated by the trigger. When the gun is cocked and a round is chambered, the firing pin is pulled back into a half-cock position. When the operator then pulls the trigger, a trigger bar pushes the striker back toward its full cock position, the bar firmly engaging with the tail of the striker. At the end of the trigger bar's journey to the rear, it comes into contact with a connector, which cams down the sear plate at the rear of the bar and thus disconnects it from the striker. At this point the striker is released and goes forward to detonate the cartridge.

The Glock firing mechanism not only reduced the number of mechanical parts, but it also reinforced the principles of simplicity that inform every aspect of the Glock design. But there is a potential problem—safety. For those familiar with firearms, the presence of a hammer can be a reassuring sight. When it is cocked it indicates that the gun is ready to go; when it is lowered it is evidently safe until the trigger is pulled. With striker-fired guns, however, there is always the looming danger a hard knock on the gun might jolt the striker onto the primer, thus resulting in an accidental discharge. Furthermore, a half-cocked striker seemed in danger of easy release should the trigger be snagged or caught. Safety was one of the key issues that

BELOW: The Glock has taken a near-starring role in many Hollywood movies, including in the hands of Jason Bourne in *The Bourne Ultimatum.*

Glock faced in gaining acceptance of his new weapon. The concerns were accentuated by the fact that the Glock, unlike almost every other brand of pistol, had no external safety lever. But safety, as it turned out, was built into the handgun at numerous levels.

First, there was the trigger. If you study the Glock trigger closely, it features an additional small plastic lever projecting from the trigger face. This is actually a trigger safety; only when the finger is fully on the trigger and depressing the safety can the gun be fired. If the lever isn't pressed in, a plastic blocking piece behind the trigger butts against the frame, and prevents the trigger moving. Second—the firing-pin safety. This consisted of a small spring-loaded pin, which projects upward into the firing pin and holds it firmly in place. Only pulling the trigger will disengage the pin from the striker and permit the gun to be fired.

The final safety mechanism on the Glock was a drop safety, a further precaution against accidental discharge. With the Glock, the cruciform sear plate at the rear of the trigger bar engages on the left with a two-level slot in the trigger mechanism housing. What this means is that only when the trigger is pulled fully to the rear can the sear plate drop into the lower portion of the slot, and only then can the striker be released forward.

BELOW: The Glock's safety trigger; if the central lever set into the trigger isn't pressed back fully with the trigger finger, the trigger can't be pulled.

Taken together, the Glock's safety mechanism provided multiple levels of reassurance, sufficient to warrant the exclusion of an external safety switch. There was a tactical implication, however. What the Glock offered was a pistol that could be carried around safely with a cartridge chambered. If the gun needed to be used, all the operator had to do was draw it, aim it, and pull the trigger, without having to stop and click off a safety switch first.

All told, the new Glock 17 was light, immensely strong, and offered a level of firepower most other handguns could not match. Now Glock simply had to persuade the rest of the world that his was the firearm of choice.

The Rise of the Glock

The Austrian Army pistol competition had a fresh face on the block. Gaston Glock, having been in firearms design and manufacturer for little more than a year, was going up against some of the mightiest names in firearms design— Heckler & Koch, Sig Sauer, Beretta, Fabrique Nationale, and Steyr. Each of the companies was fielding strong contenders for the Austrian gun, and Glock was not the only one offering high-capacity magazines. One of the rival guns, the H&K P9S, held 18 rounds.

ABOVE: An Iraqi Special Weapons and Tactics (SWAT) student fires his Glock 19 service pistol at select targets during live-fire training.

But the Glock had so many other advantages to offer, and incredibly it won the day. On November 5, 1982, Glock was informed that the Glock 17 had beaten the competition and that he was to become the official supplier of the army's new handgun. Underwriting that point in clear commercial terms, the Austrian MoD gave Glock a contract for 20,000 guns in 1983.

And yet, this was just the beginning of the epic success story on which the Glock handgun was about to embark. Although Gaston Glock was, publicly, a somewhat reticent and formal individual, he was nevertheless ambitious and circumspect, and he and his representatives quickly began to

RIGHT: These German GSG9 officers have fitted their Glocks with tactical lights/laser systems, to provide faster target acquisition in low-light conditions.

scout out more markets. Essentially, the available markets broke down into three types: civilian, law enforcement, and military. The law enforcement category was particularly important, as the weapon that a police force carried was essentially given widespread and free publicity to the civilian market. Military sales, as the Austrian Army contract had proven, also had impressive potential, but there were more commercial pitfalls—military sales typically result in very low margins per unit and they are subject to political vagaries. For Glock, this latter point was proven by his refusal to participate in the 1984 XM-9 Personal Defense Pistol Trials in the United States, the competition to replace the aging M1911 Colt as the standard handgun of the US armed forces. Despite the potentially huge volume of sales that the contract would garner, Glock backed out of the competition both because it would involve too much modification of his production processes to meet the US specifications, plus he didn't want to hand over any production rights to the US government (a condition of the competition). In the end, the Beretta 92 won that competition, but it is fair to say that Glock wouldn't go on to live with regrets.

With the Austrian Army purchase of the Glock, the rest of the world took notice and sales soon began to gather pace. The Glock had a particular appeal to special forces and elite police and security units, who appreciated its high magazine capacity, light weight, and fast-shooting characteristics. Early customers during this period included the German GSG9 counter-terrorism force, the Royal Canadian Mounted Police Urge Team, the Indian Special Protection Guard, and numerous VIP protection squads. Despite the potential pitfalls of military sales, the Glock was also doing well there. Sweden and Norway both trialed the gun in 1984–85, and like Austria, eventually adopted it as their standard side arm. As more European countries either embraced the Glock or at least showed a definite interest in it, the Model 17 was authorized as a NATO standard issue firearm, widening its potential markets.

But there was one key market that as yet was closed to Glock—the United States. Here was a ripe fruit for the picking, not least because the emergence of the Glock coincided with the point in history at which many US law enforcement agencies were looking to replace their five- or six-shot revolvers with modern semi-auto pistols packing much better firepower. People in

GLOCK 17 GEN2
DATE:
1988
CALIBER:
9 x 19mm
LENGTH:
8.03in (204mm)
BARREL LENGTH:
4.48in (114mm)
WEIGHT (LOADED):
32.12oz (910g)
MAGAZINE CAPACITY
(STANDARD):
17
RANGE
50yds (45.72m)

the United States were certainly taking notice, and Peter Kasler notes that between 1982 and 1985, not fewer than 36 US firearms importers actually contacted Glock for licenses to import the weapon into their country.

One of the key figures who facilitated the Glock's movement into the US market was Austrian émigré Karl Walter. Walter first came into contact with the Glock handgun during a business trip to Germany and Austria in 1984, in the presence of firearms journalist Peter Kokalis. They met with Gaston Glock personally, and he demonstrated the gun's virtues, which impressed the visitors. Walter suggested that Kokalis write an article about the Glock in the internationally popular *Soldier of Fortune* magazine, which would help lever the Glock into US consciousness. Cannily entitled "Plastic Perfection," the article appeared in October 1984. Some select extracts sum up the degree of respect the weapon commanded:

"The best pistol will not win the current XM9 (Personal Defense Weapon PDW) trials. The finest military pistol in the world today, in my opinion, is not entered in the XM9 tests.

Currently in service only with the Austrian Army, the revolutionary Glock 17 pistol was withheld from the U.S. XM9 trials at the behest of its inventor, Gaston Glock, who would not accept U.S. government requirements to release the winning contender's production and patent rights to open bidding. The Glock pistol represents an entirely new era in small arms technology. …

RIGHT: An Austrian Army soldier, armed with a Glock 17 on his hip, conducts a vehicle search.

Five thousand miles is a long way to travel just to shoot another 9mm pistol. But the Glock 17 is not just another pistol. I must admit, however, that my initial reaction was genuine skepticism. Is nothing sacred anymore? Now they're even making pistol frames out of plastic? In our pop culture 'plastic' has come to mean vacuous or devoid of substance. Yet, plastic is a salient feature of the Glock design. Not only the frame, but the trigger and magazine as well are made of this material.

…

Safe, reliable, accurate, instantly ready, easy to maintain, a minimal number of parts, light, compact, durable (almost indestructible), low felt recoil, a large capacity magazine, simplified training, and natural, instinctive pointing qualities— the Glock 17 possesses every single characteristic anyone has ever dreamed of having in a combat pistol. I have only one major criticism: It is not yet available in the U.S."

—Kokalis, "Plastic Perfection," *Soldier of Fortune* (October 1984)

GLOCK 17 US PRESS RELEASE—DECEMBER 1, 1985

The Glock 17 cal. 9mm para semi automatic "safe action" pistol will be available in a commercial version, early 1986 in the United States.

The Glock Inc. Distribution and future manufacturing center has been established in Smyrna, GA, to service the US commercial, law enforcement, and military markets. The Glock 17 pistol has been in production by Glock Ges.m.b.H in Austria since 1983. It has been approved and adopted by the Austrian Police and Military Forces after competing and winning against all major international and national competitors. By late 1985, the Glock 17 pistol became also NATO classified, being already introduced as the standard side arm of a NATO country, and various special police/military units and sport shooters throughout the free world.

Its popularity is growing rapidly.

The Glock 17 pistol reveals a new advanced manufacturing technology of a synthetic made (polymer) frame, magazine (17 round capacity), and other pistol parts, resulting in the use of the lowest component requirement of any pistol which, combined with the new Glock "safe action" firing mechanism, offers utmost reliability, accuracy, light weight, and shooting comfort. It operates "revolver-like" without using the conventional lateral safety lever and is, therefore, ready for firing at once with a smooth and steady trigger-pull that does not change from the first to the last round.

ABOVE: Glock runs the US side of its business from its North America headquarters in 6000 Highlands Parkway, Smyrna, Georgia.

Kokalis would not have to wait long. In July 1985, Glock submitted the Model 17 to the Bureau of Alcohol, Tobacco, and Firearms (BATF) for approval regarding importation into the United States, at the same time as Glock and his marketing manager, Wolfgang Riedl, began the process of setting up a US distribution base. The BATF required a few modifications before the gun was approved—specifically a metal serial number plate on the underside of the receiver, and an adjustable rear sight in place of the Glock's standard fixed sight. Glock responded quickly, and the gun was granted approval in November 1985. In that same month, Glock Inc. was established in Smyrna, Georgia, where it remains to this day.

The United States—Controversy and Acceptance

The Glock caught on almost immediately in the United States. Within days of the US center coming into action, it was working at about 80 percent of its capacity, a goal that Glock Inc. had forecast would take many years to reach. The largest part of the sales went to the US law enforcement community. Kasler points to the impressive facts that "by the end of 1990 there were more than 300,000 Glock pistols in use throughout North America. By April 1991, more than 3,500 federal, state, and local law enforcement agencies had issued or authorized Glock pistols for duty use, and there were 200,000 pistols in the hands of law enforcement personnel alone" (Kasler, 1992, p.12). In just one day—the first day of the National Association of Sporting Good Retailers show in Denver in December 1985—Glock took orders for 20,400 handguns. Bear in mind that Riedl and Walter had aimed to sell just 8,500 units in the entire first year, so that they could break even.

The Glock's sales explosion was assisted by the fact that because of the material and production efficiencies within the Glock's manufacture, the

gun could be sold at significantly lower prices than many of the competing weapons on the market. The wholesale price of a Glock 17 was $360, and the retail price $560, but even with the low selling price Glock was still making a margin of around 65 percent (Barrett, 2013, pp.37–38). So as well as changing the technological landscape of firearms, Glock had also redrawn the commercial landscape as well.

But this immediate meteoric rise was not a foregone conclusion, not least because there were some powerful forces arraigned against the Glock's distribution within the United States. For as soon as the Glock entered the market, figures in the US Department of Defense (DoD) and Secret Service were watching its sales and distribution carefully. There were two events that unleashed a storm of adverse, but ultimately beneficial, publicity upon the pistol and its producer.

Glock sales to the Middle East had pricked the interest of the US intelligence agencies, particularly to regimes such as Syria—Hafez al-Assad had ordered some Glocks for his presidential guard. One of those looking at the gun was Noel Koch, a DoD counter-terrorism chief, and he didn't

ABOVE: A group of US commercial pilots train in defense tactics using Glock 17 T FX pistols, which fire non-lethal marker or plastic ammunition.

like what he saw. He was concerned that the high percentage of polymer components in the weapon would render it invisible to airport radar, at a time when the world was plagued with aviation terrorism. He was also alarmed by Israeli intelligence that claimed Glocks were being sold to the pariah Libyan state of Colonel Muammar al Gaddafi, a claim that the Glock company would later strenuously deny.

Koch decided to test out his theories about the Glock and airport security, in high-risk style. He dismantled a Glock 17 into its major component parts, distributed them throughout his duffel bag, and then took the gun through the security at Washington International Airport, with no problems whatsoever. It was the catalyst for going public about the Glock, which Koch now wanted banned from importation into the United States.

On January 15, 1985, an incendiary article appeared in the *Washington Post*, written by journalists Jack Anderson and Vale Van Atta, and provocatively entitled "Qaddafi Buying Austrian Plastic Pistols." The first paragraphs of the article made their point in no uncertain terms:

"Libyan dictator Muammar Qaddafi is in the process of buying more than 100 plastic handguns that would be difficult for airport security forces to detect.

Incredibly, the pistols are made in Austria—where Qaddafi-supported terrorists shot up the Vienna airport during Christmas week. "This is crazy," one top official told us. "To let a madman such as Qaddafi have access to such a pistol! Once it is in his hands, he'll give it to terrorists throughout the Middle East."

The handgun in question is the Glock 17, a 9mm pistol invented and manufactured by Gaston-Glock in the village of Deutsch-Wagram, just outside Vienna. It is accurate, reliable, and made almost entirely of hardened plastic. Only the barrel, slide and one spring are metal. Dismantled, it is frighteningly easy to smuggle past airport security."

—*Washington Post* (January 15, 1985)

The article went on refer to "one Pentagon security expert"—Koch—who smuggled the gun undetected through the Washington airport security.

The *Post* article triggered a near-hysterical media interest in the Glock. Articles appeared in other newspapers reinforcing the points made by Anderson and Atta, and leading to new labels for the Glock, such as the "Hijacker's Special." The US government also became involved, with a special congressional review scheduled before the House of Representatives Committee on the Judiciary Subcommittee on Crime, tasked to look into the threat from "plastic pistols" and scheduled for the spring of 1986. Several police departments and even entire states issued bans on the Glock, defining it as a terrorist weapon. For a time, there was the real danger that Glock's expansion into the United States would be snuffed out even as it was just starting to form a flame.

But it was not to be, as both calmer heads and actual evidence came to prevail. Prior to the congressional hearings, at a Pentagon meeting, it was revealed that Koch actually had another, entirely different, handgun on his person during the run through the Washington International Airport security. He had a fully assembled Heckler & Koch P9 taped into his briefcase, a weapon that also sailed through the screenings without hindrance. It appeared that the problem was more to do with lax airport security than any radar-invisible properties of the Glock itself. The revelation of this fact during the hearings prompted the following official summary:

BELOW: A Glock passes through airport security in Vienna, 1986, clearly demonstrating that the Glock is far from invisible to radar.

"It was clearly pointed out that the disclosure of the true test findings could encourage mad people to test security with their guns and that this would not be in anyone's best interest; hence, no supplemental reports have been made to the media by the Pentagon Officials concerning the assembled H&K P-9 pistol in the Under Secretary's briefcase, which is approximately the same size as the Glock 17 pistol that evaded security personnel as well."

—US House of Representatives (1986): p. 205

Gaston Glock's Testimony

Part of Glock's opening statement to the House of Representatives Committee on the Judiciary Subcommittee on Crime, "Firearms that can escape detection."

"Contrary to the media reports, the Glock 17 pistol is not an entire plastic pistol. It contains 83 percent of hardened steel of its total 23 ounces (652 g), unloaded. That is more than a pound of metal, and as our submitted documentation indicate, it is clearly detectable at present airport security systems in the United States and abroad, and has not been, as of this date, used in any terrorist activity. The real difficult detectable threats, like explosives and nonmetal firearms, are as much of a concern to myself as to any individual that travels extensively by air, especially abroad. Though I am not an authority on security systems and its equipment it is

obvious to me while on international travels that airport security in other nations appears to be much stricter than here in the United States. For example, in West Germany, Austria, or Switzerland, heavily armed and well-trained Federal police officers secure airports and have at their disposal at airports antiterrorist units for emergency backup. In Tokyo, an empty cigarette pack containing a small amount of cello-foil will trip their magnetometers. Why don't ours do that? The Israeli security is known to be one of the most thorough ones worldwide. Since the beginning of the Glock 17 controversy, which we truly did not anticipate, our office in Georgia receives phone calls daily from US citizens that suggest and support legislative actions to improve security devices and training for better security personnel on Federal, State, and local levels where it might be needed, rather than prohibiting the technical advancements or availability of technical advanced firearms in the United States, that might be used in the future to defend this great symbol of freedom and democracy: the United States."

—US House of Representatives (1986): pp.184–85

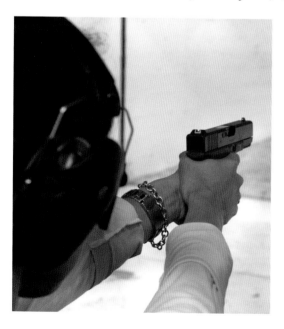

BELOW: Glocks have achieved popularity with a huge variety of users —here we see one at the Florida Firearms Academy range, during their weekly Ladies' Night.

Other evidence, including that produced by Gaston Glock during the hearings, progressively proved that the Glock was no invisible pistol and that with appropriate security technology the metal parts of the Glock would be fully revealed.

The accusations thrown during the hearings, depicting the Glock as a "Hijacker's Special," simply didn't add up in the end. Although the bill to prohibit "the importation of any firearm that is not readily detectable as a firearm by the standard security equipment commonly used at airports and readily identifiable as a firearm" subsequently entered the statute books, Glock and his advocates had squarely proved that the handgun was indeed fully detectable.

The case leveled against the Glock had been dispiriting and generally ill-informed. And, as it turned out, it actually bought the Glock millions of dollars' worth of free publicity. The hype around the pistol had given it a certain notoriety and cache, and civilian, military, and law enforcement buyers around the world began to purchase the gun in ever-increasing volumes. The stories of the military and law-enforcement use of the Glock are told in later chapters. Suffice to say here that the Glock now began its exorable rise to become America's number one handgun, as well as in the wider world.

The Glock Choice

In the next chapter, we will look in detail at each of the Glock variants. Before doing so, the overall driving forces behind the gun's technical development should be noted. The Glock does not, nor ever has, exist in a vacuum, and it has had to change to market forces like any other product. The two main driving forces in gun development are the requirements of the customer and the simultaneous requirement to beat the competitors.

ABOVE: The Glock Gen3 delivered a significant change in the Glock format by, among other things, introducing an accessory rail at the front of the frame.

For the customer, especially in the civilian and the law-enforcement communities, the chief concern behind a gun selection is to find the right match for his or her tactical, physical, and financial requirements. That means that one size simply doesn't fit all. Glock, therefore, has since the mid 1980s sought to develop a weapon series that is adaptable and versatile for a mixed society. For those who want a comfortable, accurate and fast-shooting standard 9mm pistol for personal defense, there is, for example, the Glock 17 or shorter Glock 19. If, however, they want to up the accuracy for competition shooting, they could go for a weapon like the G34, with its increased slide and barrel length and greater precision. Alternatively, you might want to go for one of Glock's many "subcompact" models, ultra-portable and discrete weapons such as the G26 and G39.

Then there is also the matter of caliber. Currently the Glock weapons are available in seven calibers—9 x 19mm, .40, 10mm Auto, .45 Auto, .45 GAP, .380 Auto, and .357—with each caliber having a specific sub-set of Glock models. In developing both the physical options for the weapons, and the range of calibers available, Glock has positioned itself to cater for almost every buyer imaginable, from a frontline soldier to a housewife wanting something for her purse.

Caliber Choice

Choice of caliber is not the most pressing of life's issues in target shooting, but for self-defense and law-enforcement use, the caliber in one's handgun is a cause of heated debate and very real relevance. The choice of caliber not only affects the size and depth of the hole that you put into a dangerous assailant, but it also affects the shooting characteristics and magazine capacity of the weapon. For example, 9mm weapons tend to give comparatively low recoil. This means the shooter can recover his point of aim more quickly between each shot, making the 9mm gun a faster-shooting proposition (with the correct training, of course).

Yet the 9mm is also one of the weaker cartridges in terms of terminal ballistics. The .45 Auto, by contrast, is a truly powerful cartridge, originally designed to drop down fanatical Moro tribesmen in the Philippines. But the wide, heavy bullet and the amount of powder required to send out the round, means that the gun kicks quite heavily, extending the between-shot recovery time unless extended training can compensate. The magazine capacity of the gun is also reduced, taking fewer of the larger rounds than the 9mm magazine.

BELOW: **An unspent 9mm cartridge is ejected from a Glock by drawing back the slide. This view clearly shows how the barrel is hinged downwards at the rear during recoil.**

Glock Series

Here it is useful to plot out some of the key landmarks in the overall evolution of the Glock series, onto which we can hang the finer details. As already noted, the Glock 17 was launched in 1983, and this model stands to this day as the foundation of the entire series, used by hundreds of thousands of individuals around the world. It is interesting to note that just three years later Glock launched the Model 18. At first glance this appeared to be a G17, but with a large manual safety switch set into the left-side slide serration. In actual fact, the G18 was a select-fire weapon that, with the flick of that switch, could go from semi-auto fire to full-auto at a cyclic rate of 1,200 rpm. It was developed specifically for the anti-terrorist officers of the Austrian EKO Cobra unit, with a detachable shoulder stock and a special 33-round extended magazine available, but it has seen relatively little practical adoption. (The availability of high-quality submachine guns such as the H&K MP5 has stolen the thunder of the G18 and many other similar selective-fire pistols.)

More significant was the release of the G19 in 1988, which was largely a G17 but with a compact frame, and corresponding reduction in the magazine capacity to 15 rounds. This handgun has been one of Glock's most popular models, particularly amongst civilian shooters wanting a self-defense handgun.

The 1990s were significant because during this decade Glock began to diversify away from the 9mm caliber. Three models in particular upped the power of the Glock range—the G20 (10mm Auto), G21 (.45 Auto), and G22 (.40)—and compact and sub-compact models of these soon followed. More calibers and models were added throughout the decade and into the 2000s, leading up to the "Gen 4"-only models such as G41 and G42. The latter, introduced in 2014 in .380 ACP caliber, and featuring a modified operating system and an ultra-compact design (magazine capacity is just six rounds), shows that the Glock guns will continue to evolve into the future.

GLOCK 18

DATE:
1985
CALIBER:
9 x 19mm
LENGTH:
7.32in (186mm)
BARREL LENGTH:
4.57in (116mm)
WEIGHT (LOADED):
22.6oz (640g)
MAGAZINE CAPACITY (STANDARD):
10, 17, 19 or 33
RANGE
55yds (50m)

Glock Generations

Against this picture of an expanding model range, we should also factor in the "generations" of evolution that have affected the Glocks. Essentially, the Glock handgun (taking the series as a whole) has gone through four "generations," signified in Glock-speak as "Gen 1," "Gen 2," etc. What these generations refer to is principally an evolution in frame design, although the Gen 4 models have taken a somewhat more radical step forward. Here is a basic guide to the Glock generations:

Gen 1—This was the first version of the gun. It can be recognized by the way that the pebbling surface goes all around the grip in unbroken fashion. These guns also have small magazine release buttons on the left side of the grip only, and a single frame pin just above the trigger.

Gen 2—Glock introduced the Gen 2 changes in 1988. The improvements were largely focused on the grip ergonomics—the wraparound pebbling was replaced with stippled panels on the sides of the grip plus checkering on the front and back straps. On the non-9mm models, an additional frame pin was added and the locking block was also enlarged, changes that were applied from 2002 to the G17, G19, and G34 models.

Gen 3—The Gen 3 configurations arrived from 1998. Here the big news was the addition of a tactical rail beneath the front of the frame (it is known officially as the "Universal Glock Rail"), for the fitment of optional equipment such as laser aiming devices and small flashlights. Providing the rail meant that Glock could compete more effectively in the heavily accessorized law-enforcement and military markets. Gen 3 guns also have a loaded chamber indicator, facilitated by the extractor. Within the Gen 3 models that was also the RTF2 sub-variants, applied specifically to the G17, G19, G22, G23, and G23C. The key characteristic of these weapons was the use of crescent-shaped slide serrations, which were intended to improve the operator's grip on the slide during cocking. (By many accounts the improvement is either negligible or non-existent.)

Gen 4—The Gen 4 Glocks were launched in 2010 to much fanfare and critical evaluation. In this generation the number and scale of the changes were far more significant. The grip circumference had been reduced overall, but the guns came with changeable backstraps to modify the grip characteristics for the individual shooter. The

BELOW: The G17C. The "C" denotes "compensated;" the cutaway aperture on the top of the slide is just visible here. Compensated models are designed to reduce muzzle recoil, making the weapon easier to control.

GLOCK 17C

DATE:
1996
CALIBER:
9 x 19mm
LENGTH:
8.03in (204mm)
BARREL LENGTH:
4.48in (114mm)
WEIGHT (LOADED):
32.12oz (910g)
MAGAZINE CAPACITY (STANDARD):
17
EFFECTIVE RANGE:
50yds (45.72m)

magazine release had become larger and more accessible, and it could also now be fitted on either side of the gun, allowing for true ambidextrous operation. The grip texture was modified, and many of the other parts received slight changes (detailed more in the next chapter). The most significant internal change was the inclusion of a captive dual-spring recoil assembly.

Through the process of generational evolution, the Glock range of handguns has kept pace with all the demands of the modern market.

Future Growth

At the very beginning of the 1990s, Glock opened a factory in South America, such was the growth in its markets there. Nor has it stopped growing since. Today it has five primary regional trading headquarters, in Austria, the United States, Hong Kong, Uruguay, and Dubai. Glock handguns are today used by more than 50 nations, in every capacity from competition shooting to frontline combat applications in major war zones.

The journey of the Glock from upstart newcomer in the 1980s to world-leading gun has been astonishing, and has few parallels in the history of modern gunmaking. Gaston Glock's personal journey has not been so smooth in recent times. This elderly billionaire has suffered two strokes, divorce from his wife, Helga, after 49 years of marriage (and remarriage to a 32-year-old nurse), an attempted murder in July 1999 (he fought off the attacker but suffered serious injuries) and various legal headaches and challenges. But what has not changed is the power of his products, the true focus of this book. At the time of writing, the British Army, for example, has signed the contract for 25,000 Glock 17 Gen4 handguns, to replace the now-dated Browning Hi-Power weapons on which it has relied for half a decade. The Glock handgun, improved but still very much connected to those first guns of the mid 1980s, continues to grab attention.

ABOVE: The Glock enjoys truly global sales—here we see a SWAT-style officer in Thailand undergoing range training with the Glock.

The 9mm Glocks

The Glock range of handguns is particularly broad, albeit recognizably anchored to the gun that set the scene, the Glock 17. A quick study of the Glock website, at the time of writing, shows a total of 49 models (if we include training pistols). The architecture of the Glock series has been explained in overview in the previous chapter. Over the course of the next three chapters, however, we will burrow down deeper and look at the characteristics that define each individual gun.

FACING PAGE: This shooter is using the G26, an ultra-compact 9 x 19mm Glock with a standard magazine capacity of 10 rounds. The gun is ideal for concealed use.

To give us a bit more navigability around the Glock range, we have arrange each of the chapters in caliber groupings, starting with the 9mm guns. And here we enter the contentious territory of caliber choice. Public debates about the optimal handgun caliber vary from the intellectually benign through to the utterly vitriolic. It is easy at least to understand the heated sentiment behind these discussions; those who might have to depend on their weapon for survival require the most effective cartridge possible, one that will put down an assailant quickly and decisively.

From the start we have to acknowledge an important myth. Contrary to almost every Hollywood movie, human beings almost never drop dead instantly when shot, unless the bullet goes through the brain itself. Instead, what typically happens is that the unfortunate individual begins to bleed with varying degrees of intensity, and if this bleeding isn't controlled by medical intervention they slip into unconsciousness and (unless treated) death from volume shock. The process can take some time, which in itself is a guiding factor behind police and military shooting techniques (see the chapter on law-enforcement Glocks). What this means for the caliber discussion is that caliber or muzzle velocity can never guarantee incapacitation in themselves.

In this regard, shot placement—the actual target area struck—is far more important than caliber. Scanning through medical histories we can find examples of individuals struck with .45 ACP cartridges in the head, yet who have both survived and thrived, against instances in which grown adults are killed by a single airgun pellet in exactly the wrong place. Yet such is not to say, of course, that caliber isn't important. Shoot a fully grown man dead center in the chest with a .22 air pellet, and the pellet is likely to stick in his sternum or bounce off a rib, with easily treated effects. Do the same with a .45 ACP, and he will likely be dead in under a minute.

BELOW: Samuel L. Jackson, in the movie *Shaft* (2000), opted for a 9mm species of Glock—the G19—as his weapon of choice.

Penetration and Cavitation

The effectiveness of a handgun ammunition type for self-defense purposes is usually judged on the basis two factors—penetration and cavitation. Penetration refers to the distance into which a bullet will penetrate before coming to a complete stop. Intuitively, we might think that ammunition designers want a round that will penetrate as deep and far as possible, but this is certainly not the case with most handgun ammunition types. The two extremes of penetration are underpenetration and overpenetration. The former means that the bullet stops too quickly to reach the vital organs that need to be affected for effective incapacitation, and is usually the result of a light bullet weight and/or a low muzzle velocity. Overpenetration means that the bullet goes through the victim and continues its flight onward rather than stops within him. Not only is that bad for bystanders, but it is also inefficient in terms of effect, as much of the bullet's energy goes into keeping it flying beyond the target, rather than dumping the energy into it. So, the ideal handgun cartridge will opt for a deep penetration but one squarely within the limits of an average human physiology. The Federal Bureau of Investigation (FBI) demands a penetration depth in ballistic gelatin (the standard material for testing cartridge penetration) as 12 inches (30cm) or greater, remembering that the depth of penetration must allow for all presentations of the target, not just face on.

Alongside penetration, however, there is cavitation. Bullets do their terrible work on human beings and animals in two essential ways. First, there is what those who specialize in terminal ballistics (the scientific study of the effect of projectiles on targets) call the "permanent cavity." This is literally a track of tissue destruction carved through the flesh by the bullet. The permanent cavity might not necessarily be a straight line of damage. Once bullets enter anything thicker than air they can tumble, bounce off solid objects (such as bone), fragment into pieces or generally go off track, so

ABOVE: The blue frame here indicates that these are G17 T FX training guns, which fire non-lethal "simunitions." These particular weapons were used as part of training with the Transportation Security Administration in Brunswick, Georgia, 2003.

the pathway can be irregular and unpredictable. Surrounding the permanent cavity is the temporary cavity. For a fraction of a second, the tissue around the bullet impact expands outward under the pressure of the bullet's shock waves. The temporary cavity thus formed is impermanent—the tissue quickly contracts back within fractions of a second—but for that brief moment it will be many times bigger than the permanent cavity it surrounds. The significance of the temporary cavity largely depends on where it takes place in the body. Inelastic or particularly sensitive organs, such as the bladder and brain, can be severely damaged by temporary cavitation, but in most cases the permanent cavity is the deciding factor in the bullet's effect.

Penetration and cavitation (both types) are byproducts of the bullet's caliber (the wider the bullet, the wider the permanent cavity), weight, and velocity. The scientific interrelationship between all these factors is complex and open to debate, but many have felt the solution is clear—you want a

ABOVE: In 2012 Glock introduced an optional color of frame, designated Flat Dark Earth (FDE). Glock had also produced a short-lived series of frames in Olive Drab Green (ODG).

large-caliber bullet with lots of power behind it to do the job. Yet as always, there are complicating factors. We already noted in Chapter 1, for example, that choosing a hefty caliber like a .45 ACP tends to reduce the number of cartridges available in the magazine, compared to say a 9mm gun, and makes it harder to put shots onto the target in rapid succession. This means that a shooter might only be able to fire two .45 ACP bullets into the target in the time it takes for another shooter to deliver four 9mm rounds, meaning that the 9mm gun actually inflicts an overall greater width and depth of permanent cavities than the heavier gun. But cartridge for cartridge, the .45 ACP with deliver a more powerful injury mechanism than the 9mm, depending on shot placement, which in turn hangs upon the skill of the individual wielding the gun.

You are probably getting a sense by now that caliber choice is a complex equation, in which improving one factor can have a negative effect on another. Hence the debates still thrive, despite decades of scientific research in both law enforcement and military medicine, and it looks set to continue for the future. What a lot of the issue boils down to is personal choice on the part of the user, and such is why Glock, like all other major gunmakers, produces its firearms in a range of popular calibers.

The 9 x 19mm Cartridge

The 9 x 19mm cartridge, often referred to as the 9mm Parabellum, is one of the most influential cartridge types in all firearms history. It is used in the majority of law-enforcement and military handguns around the world today (as well as the vast majority of the world's submachine guns), offering as it does a useful combination of characteristics—practical performance in terms of velocity, penetration, and cavitation; a very low unit cost; and easily controlled recoil. Its origins reach back into the early years of the 20th century, when it was developed by the famous German gunmaker Georg Luger for his new range of pistols. Actually creating the cartridge was a simple matter of removing the bottleneck section of Luger's 7.65 x 21mm Parabellum, to take it up to 9mm (0.354in). The resulting cartridge offered a more powerful option to the smaller cartridges then prevalent, but it kept the recoil manageable and it quickly appealed to both military and civilian clients.

BELOW: The Beretta M9 is a military spec Beretta 92F, and is currently the US armed services standard-issue 9mm handgun.

The 9mm Parabellum steadily rose to dominance among its market sectors during the first half of the 1900s, especially among European clients. The leaning toward heavier, more powerful .45 cartridges in pistols and submachine guns in the United States meant that it would take more time to catch on there. In fact, even today the 9mm is regarded as a somewhat "weak" cartridge by many in the United States (erroneously), and some also in Europe, although the sheer ubiquity of its use in combat should surely have put such reservations to rest. Nor has the 9mm stayed still in terms of development. The production of specialist hollow-point and expanding varieties such the end of World War II has given the 9mm some powerful options for increasing the cavitation effects on the target. Furthermore, velocities have increased respectably due to the emergence, since the 1990s, of new extra-power loadings, featuring high-performance powders and heavier bullets. These cartridges are designated either +P or (for even more power) +P+, and each delivers a higher muzzle velocity than a standard 9mm cartridge. Thus while a Browning Hi-Power during the 1950s would have generated a muzzle velocity of about 1,110 feet per second (335 m/sec), today's Glock firing a +P or +P+ load can deliver a round at up to around 1,350 feet per second (410 m/sec). Penetration figures have also increased from around 10–12 inches (250–305mm) to nearly 16 inches (406mm) of

BELOW: **The Glock 17 is the foundation model for the entire Glock series, and it remains one of the most popular models in the Glock range.**

ballistic gelatin. Through such advances, it can no longer be said that the 9mm is a weak round, hence it has been and continues to be adopted by armies and police forces. Such is why Glock has always offered some of its core models in 9mm Parabellum.

Glock 17

Earlier we looked at the general technical properties of the Glock 17, and that information will not be repeated again here. What we will do is explore the Glock's dimensions, build, and functionality a little more closely.

One thing that we notice straight away about the Glock 17 is its very "flat" profile, courtesy of the bar-cut rectangular slide. The total height of the gun is 5.43 inches (138mm). Comparing this against the 5.5 inches (140mm) of the Beretta M9, the US military version of the Beretta M92, is revealing. The Glock manages to be 0.08 inches (2mm) more compact in height than the Beretta, but at the same time manages to pack another two 9mm rounds into the magazine. Interestingly, in the very earliest models of the Glock 17 the slide was actually somewhat narrower than what became the standard type, on account of a tighter barrel boring. These versions of the Glock are referred to as "pencil barrel" types, production of which stopped many years ago.

	GLOCK 17	GLOCK 17 GEN4
CALIBER:	9 x 19mm	9 x 19mm
LENGTH:	8.03in (204mm)	7.95in (202mm)
HEIGHT:	5.43in (138mm)	5.43in (138mm)
WIDTH:	1.18in (30mm)	1.18in (30mm)
LENGTH BETWEEN SIGHTS:	6.49in (165mm)	6.49in (165mm)
BARREL HEIGHT:	1.26in (32mm)	1.26in (32mm)
BARREL LENGTH:	4.48in (114mm)	4.48in (114mm)
WEIGHT (UNLOADED):	25.06oz (710g)	25.06oz (710g)
WEIGHT (LOADED):	32.12oz (910g)	32.12oz (910g)
TRIGGER PULL:	~5.5lb (~2.5kg)	~5.5lb (~2.5kg)
TRIGGER TRAVEL:	~0.49in (~12.5mm)	~0.49in (~12.5mm)
BARREL RIFLING:	right hand, hexagonal	right hand, hexagonal
RIFLING LENGTH OF TWIST:	9.84in (250mm)	9.84in (250mm)
MAGAZINE CAPACITY (STANDARD):	17	17
MAGAZINE CAPACITY (OPTIONAL):	10/33	10/33

RIGHT: The G17 Gen4.
The Gen4 have a number
of significant improvements
when compared to the
Gen1 series, including
better ergonomics and
ambidextrous handling.

GLOCK 17 GEN4

DATE:
2010
CALIBER:
9 x 19mm
LENGTH:
7.95in (202mm)
BARREL LENGTH:
4.48in (114mm)
WEIGHT (LOADED):
32.12oz (910g)
MAGAZINE CAPACITY
(STANDARD):
17
RANGE
50yds (45.72m)

The flat configuration and squat profile of the slide offers some advantages to the shooter. The recoil plane is kept low to the shooter's grip hand, making the gun more controllable when delivering quick shots. At 6.49 inches (165 mm) the sight radius is longer than many other guns, such as the M1911. What this means in practical terms is that the Glock is an accurate gun, within the limitations of the handgun type.

The Glock 17's barrel length runs to 4.49 inches (114mm), which with the 9mm round helps deliver a muzzle velocity of 1,230 feet per second (375 m/sec). The barrel itself is hammer forged, with right-hand twist polygonal rifling and a length of twist of 9.84 inches (250mm). Unlike many handguns, the Glock series avoids the lands and grooves of traditional rifling, the equivalent being smooth undulations, produced by beating a rotating mandrel down through the bore. Not many other handguns use this configuration, but the gas seal around the bullet is excellent, meaning that the handgun delivers ballistic efficiency.

The angle of the Glock 17's grip was one of the early issues for debate when the handgun was first being designed. Glock ultimately opted for an angle from the vertical of 22 degrees; in most other handguns the angle is about 18 degrees. The angle of the grip is highly relevant to an appreciation of any Glock, and its effect on handling will be studied in depth later. Suffice to say here that by angling the grip back a little more compared to other handguns, Glock designed a weapon that the user could "punch" onto target quickly and without much considered aim. The standard sights consist of two fixed posts to the rear, the gap between aligned with a square front post. All posts have white circles on them, to aid with low-light shooting. There are some other sighting options available, however (see below).

The Glock 17 is a light gun—25 ounces (710g) empty—thanks to its extensive use of polymer materials. The weight climbs to 32 ounces (910g) once the Glock has been loaded with a 17-round magazine. Note that there are 10-round and 33-round magazine options for the Glock, but the 17-round version is by far the most commonly used.

Magazine Types

Which brings us to the issue of magazines. As with many Glock components, even the magazine has been the subject of scrutiny and controversy, the debate often reflecting a somewhat different approach to hand gunning between the Europeans and the Americans. When the Glock was originally launched, the magazine had a distinctive "non-drop" configuration. By this, I mean that when the user presses the magazine-release button, the magazine doesn't slide out under its own weight—instead the user has to extract the magazine manually by gripping its baseplate and drawing it out. This is in contrast to the more familiar drop magazine, which falls out of the gun under the force of gravity alone when the magazine release is pressed. Non-drop magazines, generally speaking, are better for those who want a more careful use of the gun, and a considered retention of the empty magazine, while drop magazines are preferred by some needing a very fast magazine change through multiple mags.

The reason for the Glock's non-drop magazines lies in the nature of the magazine's construction. In most handguns, magazines are formed by rigid steel tubes, which have limited frictional grip against the sides of the

BELOW: A Glock user prepares to drive a 17-round magazine up into a G17; ideally the muzzle of the gun should be pointing away from the body during loading.

GLOCK 17L
DATE:
1988
CALIBER:
9 x 19mm
LENGTH:
8.86in (225mm)
BARREL LENGTH:
6.02in (153mm)
WEIGHT (EMPTY):
23.6oz (670g)
MAGAZINE CAPACITY (STANDARD):
17
EFFECTIVE RANGE:
55yds (50m)

magazine well. In the Glock, by contrast, the magazine was formed by first creating a three-sided inner tube from sheet metal, to hold the cartridges at the sides and on the front, then wrapping this structure in the polymer material to enclose it. By having a three-sided metal liner, which by its very nature has flex rather than the rigidity of a four-sided design, plus a somewhat malleable polymer coating, the magazine would press out to grip the walls of the magazine well even when the mag release button had been pressed.

Non-drop magazines are still available for those who want them, but a poor reception to this configuration from many in the US market led to the introduction of drop types as well. In these, the internal metal magazine tube is four-sided and rigid, meaning that the magazine doesn't flex out like the other type, and hence can drop out freely when required. The key visual distinction between the drop and none-drop magazines is that the former have a square-edged U-shaped notch at the rear of the feed lips, whereas the notch on the latter is a smooth U-shape.

The impressive magazine capacity is produced by virtue of slightly wider and longer magazine than many other guns, plus high shoulders to the feed lips. A useful feature of the Glock magazines is a series of numbered apertures on the rear, which show at a glance the number of cartridges still left in the magazine, should the operator want to perform a top-up.

Returning our focus to the gun itself, one interesting sub-variant of the Glock 17 is the Model 17L, the first of Glock's competition models. Particularly in the United States, combat handgun competitions are hugely popular, and Glock needed a version designed specifically for the additional accuracy and handling requirements. The Glock 17L, released in 1988, differed principally from the G17 through having a longer slide and barrel—the barrel extends an additional 1.5 inches (38mm) compared to the standard G17 barrel—fitted to a standard G17 frame, although the slide is machined slightly differently to keep the gun weight down. The principal effects of this configuration are to give a marginally higher muzzle velocity, better bullet stabilization and, most importantly, a longer sight radius, improving the accuracy of the shooting. Glock 17Ls, however, are now something of a rarity, as changes in the scoring and rules of competition shooting meant that more handgunners gravitated to non-9mm guns, in which Glock offered its own ranges (see below).

If anyone might doubt the efficacy of Glocks as competition guns, compared to some of the more precision options out there, the example of Miami police officer Armando Valdes offers a corrective. In October 1990, Valdes was competing in the World Shoot IX Championships in Adelaide, Australia. The competition was exacting, with some of the world's best handgun shooters competing over the course of nine days, and in 29 events. Valdes was equipped with a Glock 17L, still a new gun at that stage in history, through which he put 300 rounds during the Stock (Production) Class event and went on to secure 1st place against 21 other shooters in the class. Kasler notes that set in the overall context of the 306 shooters who competed, Valdes's scores placed him and the Glock in the top 12 percent.

Glock 19

The Glock 17, now having evolved to the Gen 4 standard, remains an extremely popular Glock model for both professionals and civilians. However, the Glock 17 is not an especially small handgun, and Glock soon sensed that a more compact version would be appreciated by the various markets. The law-enforcement community was a natural focus, as it is one of the few groups of people who have to carry a handgun around for the entirety of their working day. Shaving a few ounces off the Glock 17 and reducing its dimensions slightly would make sense for many in this community.

The Glock 19, released onto the market in 1988, is one of what Glock refers to as its "compact" models. (At the time of writing, these consist of the Glock 19, G23, G25, G32, and G38, with all but the Glock 25 and Glock 38 having Gen4 variants.) All the key dimensions of the gun are reduced. Compared to the G17, the frame is 0.43 inches (11mm) shorter, the barrel is 0.47 inches (12mm) shorter, as is the slide. The butt height is also shorter, to the tune of 0.43 inches (11mm), and this naturally means a reduction in the magazine capacity to 15 rounds as standard.

However, it should be noted that the G19, as with many other Glocks, doesn't need to be restricted to the factory-provided magazine. In fact, it can take the standard 17-round G17 magazines, although with an obvious baseplate projection from the bottom of the stock, or the 15-round magazines can be fitted with +2 extensions. For those requiring heavier payloads of ammunition, there are options for magazines up to 33 rounds capacity, with some options between depending on the extension fitting. Yet fitting larger magazines somewhat defeats the purpose of the original purchase, given that the handgun is designed for concealability and weight reductions. The weight savings between the G17 and G19 are not huge, but they are

GLOCK 19
DATE:
1988
CALIBER:
9 x 19mm
LENGTH:
7.36in (187mm)
BARREL LENGTH:
4.01in (102mm)
WEIGHT (EMPTY):
23.65oz (670g)
MAGAZINE CAPACITY
(STANDARD):
15
EFFECTIVE RANGE:
50yds (45.72m)

noticeable. While the G17, unloaded, weighs in at 25.06 ounces (710g), the Glock 19 weighs 23.65 ounces (670g).

There are some very subtle differences in performance between the G17 and G19. The latter has a slightly lower muzzle velocity plus, on account of the shorter barrel, a slightly higher muzzle blast and recoil. These are not highly accented, however, and many shooters find that simply replacing their preferred G17 ammunition with a slightly softer-shooting cartridge approximates the feel of the G17 anyway. It is admittedly not the best competition gun, as the shortening of the slide naturally results in the shortening of the sight radius, meaning that it offers slightly poorer accuracy (only significant for precision target shooting). For this reason, the G19s in their standard configuration are not very common competition guns, although custom precision sights can be fitted in place of the rear notch, with some machining involved. The G19s have been very well received by the law-enforcement and self-protection markets, however, both appreciating the compact portability of the weapon and its still respectable magazine capacity.

ABOVE: **This G19 is fitted with the ultimate firepower option for Glocks—an extended magazine holding no fewer than 33 rounds of 9mm ammunition.**

Suppressors

The G19 has undergone the generational improvement of all the other
models, and its Gen4 iteration is an impressive piece of kit. The only key
dimensional difference between it and the original G19, however, is in
terms of the length—7.28 inches (185mm) as opposed to the earlier gun's
7.36 inches (187mm). Like the other Gen4 guns, they can take a variety of
tactical fittings to the slide rail beneath the muzzle, and we will say more
about these options during the course of the book. Yet one very recent

LEFT: The G19, being an officially "compact" version of the G17, has proved especially popular with both law-enforcement and military units, being easier to handle than the G17 for those with smaller hands. (The gun here is an Airsoft version.)

development that requires special mention is the capacity to fit the Gen3 G19—along with the Gen3 G17, G21 SF, and G23—with suppressors.

The legal status of silenced handguns varies wildly according to where you live in the world. In some countries, just owning a handgun will get you many years in prison, and adding a silencer to the mix will simply serve to increase your sentence. However, in the United States silencers can be purchased in certain states, providing you can jump through many legal hoops put in place by the ATF.

GLOCK 19C
DATE:
1988
CALIBER:
9 x 19mm
LENGTH:
7.36in (187mm)
BARREL LENGTH:
4.01in (102mm)
WEIGHT (EMPTY):
23.6oz (670g)
**MAGAZINE CAPACITY
(STANDARD):**
15
EFFECTIVE RANGE:
50yds (45.72m)

FACING PAGE: Glock 19 handguns shown in their Gen3 and Gen4 configurations.

BELOW: This G19 has been accessorized with a GTL 10 tactical light system, clipping onto the underbarrel rail.

Suppressors—or "silencers"—work by containing and controlling the muzzle blast of a gun, reducing the auditory signature of firing to a hefty "thump" rather than no sound at all. To take an optional (rather than integral) silencer, a gun requires a threaded muzzle. Glock threaded barrels are given the designation "TB," and being manufactured in Austria they come with a metric left-hand thread pattern: 13.5 x 1 for the G17, G19, and G23 barrels and 16 x 1 for the G21 SF. The threaded portion adds 0.5 inches (13mm) to the length of the standard barrel, the section protecting visibly out from the front of the slide.

Fitting the TB is simplicity itself. The gun's slide is removed and the standard barrel replaced with the TB—no special modification for recoil or ammunition type is required. The gun is put back together and one of a selection of commercially available suppressors can now be screwed onto the thread. The noise reduction is immediately appreciable, especially if the user opts for a sub-sonic ammunition type. (Much of the noise of a gun firing is due to the bullet breaking the sound barrier, so sub-sonic rounds specially cater for suppressed weaponry.) The one problem with fitting a TB to a standard

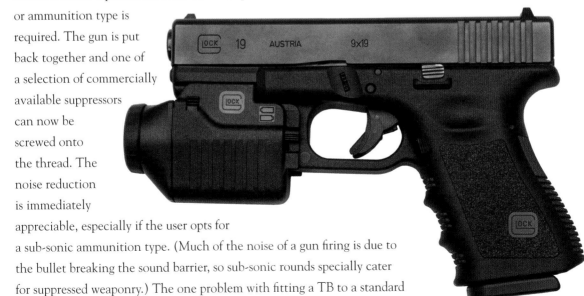

Glock can be that the circumference of the suppressor actually interferes with the sight picture. Glock has thought of this by providing TB handguns with elevated rear sights, to "look over" the suppressor. Using these sights and good ammunition, a well-trained shooter should be able to produce sub 2 inch (50mm) groups at ranges of 25 yards (23m).

RIGHT: A diagram of the G19 fitted with the extended 33-round magazine. Note the double-stack arrangement of the cartridges internally.

RIGHT: A Lone Wolf 9mm barrel, threaded at the muzzle end for taking a suppressor if required.

Glock 26

Glock has
appreciated that
for some individuals even the dimensions
of the "Compact" range are too large.
What such shooters typically require is the
ultimate in pocket power, a weapon that can
sit snugly in a low-visibility holster or which can drop
into a small backpack or handbag. It is for this reason that Glock has also
developed the "subcompact" range, which at the time of writing consists of
the G26, G27, G28, G29, G30, G33, and G39 (standard and Gen4), making
the range more extensive than any of the other types. In 9mm caliber, the
subcompact gun is the G26, which was introduced into the market in 1994.

In some ways, the Glock 26 tackles the revolver in its own backyard.
Consider this. The Glock 26 is just 6.41 inches (163mm) long and weighs
21.71 ounces (615 g) unloaded, shorter and lighter than many police-
issue revolvers, but packing a 10-round magazine, with options for 17- and
33-round mags plus the effectiveness of the 9mm round. This package means
that the G26 offers a handgun that is intermediate between a stumpy short-
barrel .38 revolver and a fully fledged semi-auto like the G17.

The G26 is focused squarely on being portable, both in terms of its
dimensions and in subtle but appreciable features such as the front of the
frame being beveled to allow the gun to slip more easily into a holster. Being
compact is good for concealability, but it can also present problems for those
who have hands on the larger side. Even individuals with medium-sized
hands will find their little fingers dropping below the magazine baseplate
on the G26, such is its size. This is not necessarily a problem—the grip
dynamics can be adjusted so that the little finger generates an upward
squeeze on the gun to deliver extra stability. However, with the magazine

GLOCK 26 Gen4

DATE:
2010
CALIBER:
9 x 19 Safe Action
LENGTH:
6.41in (163mm)
BARREL LENGTH:
3.42in (87mm)
WEIGHT (LOADED):
26.12oz (740g)
**MAGAZINE CAPACITY
(STANDARD):**
10
EFFECTIVE RANGE:
50yds (45.72m)

	GLOCK 26	GLOCK 26 GEN4
CALIBER:	9 x 19mm	9 x 19mm
LENGTH:	6.41in (163mm)	6.41in (163 mm)
HEIGHT:	4.17in (106mm)	4.17in (106mm)
WIDTH:	1.18in (30mm)	1.18in (30mm)
LENGTH BETWEEN SIGHTS:	5.39in (137mm)	5.39in (137mm)
BARREL HEIGHT:	1.26in (32mm)	1.26in (32mm)
BARREL LENGTH:	3.42in (87mm)	3.42in (87mm)
WEIGHT (UNLOADED):	21.71oz (615g)	21.71oz (615g)
WEIGHT (LOADED):	26.12oz (740g)	26.12oz (740g)
TRIGGER PULL:	~5.5lb (~2.5kg)	~5.5lb (~2.5kg)
TRIGGER TRAVEL:	0.49in (~12.5mm)	0.49in (~12.5mm)
BARREL RIFLING:	right hand, hexagonal	right hand, hexagonal
RIFLING LENGTH OF TWIST:	9.84in (250mm)	9.84in (250mm)
MAGAZINE CAPACITY (STANDARD):	10	10
MAGAZINE CAPACITY (OPTIONAL):	15/17/33	15/17/33

BELOW: In its dimensions, the G26 is actually little different from a snub-nosed .38-caliber revolver.

extensions fitted, or using the higher-capacity standard options, the magazine can act as a grip extension, albeit one that doesn't want to take too much grip strain, to avoid placing the magazine feed under tension.

Internally, the G26 does have a few differences from the other Glocks, in order to handle the shortened dimensions. The chief of these is the recoil spring. Because of slide shortening, the gun needs a more compact recoil spring system in order to pass through its full cycle after firing. To accomplish this, Glock has used a dual-spring telescoping spring system, rather than the single spring fitted into the larger guns. (A single coil spring would be too thick and too long to work inside the frame of the G26.) What this means, however, is that the gun has to deliver plenty of kick to cycle effectively. Glock experts such as Patrick Sweeney (his *Gun Digest Book of the Glock* is highly recommended) note that the G26 really requires the use of "hot" (+P or +P+) ammunition to ensure that the weapon smartly drives the slide backward, sufficient to allow good cartridge extraction and ejection. If the cartridge doesn't carry sufficient punch, then the result can be spent cases not clearing the weapon and jamming between the slide and the ejection port when the gun attempts to return to battery.

Glock 34

We have already seen, in the G17L, how the Glock can be configured for competition shooting. The 17L is far from alone in the Glock range, as there are several other competition shooting options, crossing the various calibers. The 9mm variant is the G34, which was introduced in 1988.

Competition handgun shooters are a generally fastidious breed, demanding a lot from their guns to inch ahead on the scoreboards. First, and most obvious, they require a gun that has ballistic accuracy, with a high standard of barrel to put shots into the target rapidly and consistently. Generally speaking, the competition shooter wants a gun with the maximum permissible barrel length; the longer the barrel, the higher the velocity of the bullet, the flatter its trajectory and, therefore, the more accurate the shot placement. Sights are also naturally important. On competition guns these can be standard fixed types, but more commonly they have adjustable rear sight blocks or even, depending on the competition, optical sights such as reflex or red-dot types. In terms of the general operability of the gun, the shooter wants a weapon that handles recoil well, so the shooter can keep the between-shot recovery time to an absolute minimum, plus the gun has

GLOCK 34

DATE:
2010
CALIBER:
9 x 19mm
WEIGHT (LOADED):
32.83oz (930g)
LENGTH:
8.81in (224mm)
BARREL LENGTH:
5.31in (135mm)
WEIGHT (UNLOADED):
25.77oz (730g)
MAGAZINE CAPACITY
(STANDARD):
17
MAGAZINE CAPACITY
(OPTIONAL):
10/33

GLOCK 34 GEN4

DATE:
2010
CALIBER:
9 x 19mm
WEIGHT (LOADED):
33.01oz (935g)
LENGTH:
8.74in (222mm)
BARREL LENGTH:
5.31in (135mm)
WEIGHT (UNLOADED):
25.95oz (735g)
MAGAZINE CAPACITY
(STANDARD):
17
MAGAZINE CAPACITY
(OPTIONAL):
10/33

to have a ergonomic smoothness, sitting comfortably in the shooter's hand and not losing that comfort over the course of potentially hundreds of shots. Finally, whatever gun the shooter opts to use, it must meet the competition criteria. These can be very tight. In the extremely popular International Practical Shooting Confederation disciplines, for example, whatever handgun is used has to fit, literally, inside a box of fixed dimensions—8.85 x 5.9 x 1.77 inches (225 x 150 x 45 mm). If the gun cannot be slotted into the box (with the gun slide up against the long edge of the box), then it can't be entered into the competition.

To create the G34, in essence Glock took the G17 frame and mounted it with a longer barrel—5.31 inches (135mm)—and corresponding slide. By lengthening the slide, the distance between the sights climbs up to 7.55 inches (192mm), giving the gun greater "pointability" compared to the non-competition models. (More about the set-up and performance of the Glock sights will be considered in the chapter on Glock handling.) However, Glock also recognized that forging a long slide and barrel means more weight for the shooter to handle in the dynamic circumstances of a competition shoot. With this in mind, there is a cut-out section on the top of the slide, at the front, to reduce the weight slightly—the G34 comes in at a manageable 25.77 ounces (730g) unloaded or 32.83 ounces (930g) with a full 17-round magazine.

The G34's handling resembles that of all Glocks, although the trigger has adjustments typical of a competition gun. While the actual operating mechanism is the standard Glock type, the trigger pull is dropped to ~4.5 pound (~2.0kg); length of pull stays the same. For magazines, the G34 takes the G17 17-round mag as standard, although 10-round and 33-round magazines are optional. All told, the G34 stacks up to a respectable competition handgun, one that has won some high-profile competitions, and will doubtless continue to do so.

Glock 18

Before moving away from the Glock 9mm weapons, there is one rather anomalous Glock weapon we need to consider—the Glock 18. In short, the Glock 18 is a selective-fire handgun—basically a machine pistol—with the capacity to fire either semi-auto or full-auto at a ferocious cyclical rate of around 1,100–1,200rpm. A burst will empty the Glock's special 33-round magazine in less than a second.

The Glock is not the first or only manufacturer to produce such weapons, but for good reason they have had limited adoption and use. In the case of the G18, it was actually produced for a specific client, the Austrian *Einsatzkommando Cobra* (EKO Cobra) counter-terrorism team, part of the Federal Ministry of the Interior. The gun emerged in 1986—the 1980s were an era known for the quest to produce heavy firepower in tiny packages. It was recognizably a Glock handgun; in fact it was largely a G17 with the selective-fire function built into it, although many of the parts between the G17 and G18 are not interchangeable.

The most noticeable difference between the G17 and G18 is the thumb-operated selector switch on the left-hand side of the receiver, with the up position giving semi-auto fire, and the down position delivering full-auto. As noted above, the rate of fire is especially brisk at 1,100–1,200 rpm, putting it in the same territory as the Micro Uzi. However, unlike the Micro Uzi, which has an integral stock and more substantial dimensions, the G18 is purely a handgun. To give it some stabilization, there is the option for a

GLOCK 18C

DATE:
2010
CALIBER:
9 x 19mm
LENGTH:
7.32in (186mm)
BARREL LENGTH:
4.57in (116mm)
WEIGHT (EMPTY):
1.36lb (.62kg)
MAGAZINE CAPACITY (STANDARD):
17
EFFECTIVE RANGE:
50yds (45.72m)

LEFT: A G18 delivers a
full-auto burst, stabilization
coming from a light metal
adjustable skeleton stock.

skeleton-arm detachable stock fitted to the bottom of the pistol grip, which
when combined with a solid two-handed grip does give the weapon the
capacity to make reasonable 3–5-round groups at 27 yards (25m). To combat
muzzle climb, some of the G18s came with vented or ported barrels, the ports
providing a directional gas resistance against the muzzle climb.

Yet ultimately, measures such as a detachable stock and vented barrel were
pushing against the inevitable reality that full-auto handguns are essentially
impractical from the outset. Submachine guns perform this role far better,
being more controllable, more accurate, having higher muzzle velocities and
penetration, and greater magazine capacities.

The Glock 18 is not displayed among the models on the current Glock
website. After supplying some to law-enforcement agencies in the United
States, Austria, and elsewhere during the 1980s, they largely fell from use as
people opted for submachine guns such as the Uzi and the MP5. With the
very strict limitations on the sale of full-auto weapons, furthermore, the G18
does not present a very convincing commercial model. Nevertheless, G18s
can be found and fired, and (to the author's knowledge) still ordered from
Glock as special purchases.

The .40 and 10mm Glocks

In January 1990, something of a revolution hit the world of handgun ammunition. For this was the year in which Smith & Wesson, working with Winchester, unveiled the .40 S&W cartridge, as an alternative to the less powerful 9mm and the more powerful .45 ACP.

FACING PAGE: A police officer from Northern Ireland fires a Glock handgun at the SWAT events at the World Police and Fire Games.

The story behind the development of this cartridge is somewhat complicated, so will be necessarily abbreviated here. In the later 1980s, the FBI began a quest to replace its service handguns, and commissioned S&W and Winchester to develop an optimal cartridge. The new cartridge had to offer 12–18 inches (30–46cm) of penetration into ballistic gelatin, but also be able to fit in sufficient quantity in high-capacity magazines. Specifically, the FBI wanted the new cartridge to reflect the performance of a 10mm reduced load ammunition trialed by the bureau.

The cartridge that emerged, the .40 S&W, shook up the handgun market to the core, particularly in the field of law-enforcement weapons. Offering the same ballistic performance as the .38-40 Winchester (the two calibers carry the same bullet weight, bullet diameter, and muzzle velocity), the .40 seemed to promise perfection. First, its 0.42 ounce (12g, 180-grain) bullet significantly outweighed the 0.28 ounce (8g, 124-grain) bullet of the 9mm, but retained a respectable muzzle velocity in

BELOW: The .40 S&W cartridge changed the landscape of law-enforcement firearms, offering an ideal mid ground between the 9mm and .45.

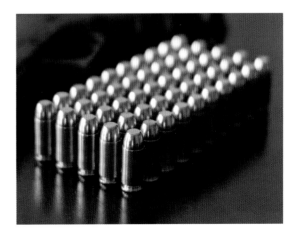

comparison—950 feet per second (290 m/sec) compared to 1,150 feet per second (350m/sec). It could deliver more ballistic energy that the .45 ACP but—and here was the clincher—the case diameter of 0.42 inches (10.8mm) meant that the cartridge was only marginally broader than the 9mm, meaning that high-capacity guns were still an option with the new round.

It was clear that the .40 S&W was going to shake things up for handgun manufacturers like Glock.

But here Glock showed its commercial stamina and initiative once again. Despite the fact that Smith & Wesson displayed a new handgun, the 11-round Model 4006, at the same time as it revealed the cartridge, it was actually a little slow in getting these guns to market. (In time, the gun would be adopted by agencies such as the California Highway Patrol, the California State Patrol, and the PA State Constables in Wisconsin.) Seizing the opportunity, Glock quickly bought out its own .40 gun, the G22, and therefore quickly stole a march on the market. Given that Glock had already a lot of momentum behind its brand, the .40-caliber guns sold extremely well, especially to police forces.

GLOCK 22
DATE:
1990
CALIBER:
.40
LENGTH:
8.03in (204mm)
BARREL LENGTH:
4.49in (114mm)
WEIGHT (LOADED):
34.42oz (975g)
MAGAZINE CAPACITY (STANDARD):
15
EFFECTIVE RANGE:
50yds (45.72m)

Glock 22

The G22 was largely a G17, but with
some features beefed-up to take the
additional power of the .40-caliber
round. Specifically, the slide was
heavier to the tune of 1.1 ounce
(31g), which imparted an additional
inertia to the recoil. At the same
time, the gun featured a more
resistant recoil spring. This feature
was actually a compensation for the
G22's lighter barrel, a measure to
keep the gun's weight to manageable
levels, which was important if Glock

was to convince law enforcement agencies to walk around with the gun on
their hips all day. Patrick Sweeney notes that overall the G22 has a four
percent greater unlocking mass than the G17. The magazine capacity was
only slightly reduced for the new caliber—15 rounds as standard instead
of 17, although with the option for fitting 10-round or 33-round mags as
required. Because of its release date, the G22 skipped the first-generation
iteration of the frame and came with the second-generation grip design.

The Glock 22 was an immediate hit, and during the 1990s and early
2000s it was adopted by many law-enforcement agencies. The latest Gen4
models remain a popular part of the Glock line, benefitting from all the
latest modern advantages—such as the new textured frame, the enlarged and
ambidextrous magazine catch, the dual recoil spring (which improves both
the recoil experience and the durability of the system against wear and tear),
and the customizable Modular Back Strap (MBS). Plus the gun has the Gen3
accessory rail beneath the muzzle.

This short explanation of the G22 rather glosses over some of the problems
that were faced by the gun and its users, particularly during the early years
of the G22's production and adoption. For although the G22 had some
engineering adaptations to cope with the more potent .40 round, in many
ways it was just a G17 that had more thump both to deliver and handle.
There was some peening (impact damage) to the lower part of the slide, the
result of the gun flexing under recoil and causing the locking block in the
frame to strike against the slide. The problem appeared to reduce after the

GLOCK 22 Gen4
DATE:
2010
CALIBER:
.40
LENGTH:
7.95in (202mm)
BARREL LENGTH:
4.49in (114mm)
WEIGHT (LOADED):
34.42oz (975g)
MAGAZINE CAPACITY
(STANDARD):
15
MAGAZINE CAPACITY
(OPTIONAL):
10/22
EFFECTIVE RANGE:
50yds (45.72m)

gun was "worn in" from firing, but Glock has also recently introduced some slide beveling to cope with the issue. The impact between locking block and slide also caused, in some cases, the locking-block pin to sheer. The introduction of dual pins solved this problem.

One interesting point to note about the .40 Glocks is that their bores and chambers have slightly broader dimensions than many other .40-caliber guns. What this means in practical terms is that on firing the cartridges swell up more to achieve obturation (the gas-tight seal between the cartridge and the walls of the chamber). While not a problem in itself for the gun, it can be an issue for those wanting to reload spent brass, as the expansion of the shell cases makes them unfit for reuse.

FACING PAGE: A Canadian policeman with his holstered Glock. Many Canadian forces have adopted the G22.

Glock 23 and 27

As with the G17's compact and subcompact offspring—the G19 and G26—the G22 was also the foundation for two smaller models. The G23 was literally a .40-caliber G19, with the magazine able to take 13 rounds as standard. The overall length was a stocky 7.36 inches (187mm), but this was easily surpassed by the G27, which dropped the length down to 6.49 inches (165mm). The magazine capacity of this gun was, during the period of the Assault Weapons Ban 1994 (1994–2004) just nine rounds for civilians, with law-enforcement officers about to carry 11. However, looking at the current Glock website the options for ammunition carry have now flowered, and include 13-, 15-, and 22-round magazines.

BELOW: A G23 is the "compact" model in Glock's .40 range, with an overall length of 7.28 inches (185mm).

As with the other subcompact models, the G27 features the double recoil spring configuration, but the G27's small frame means that it requires a shooter with a strong wrist to keep the gun on target through rapid fire. Note that Glock also produced a ported-barrel version, the G27C, to offset, to some degree, the heavy kick of the .40 round from the diminutive gun.

RIGHT: The G23 Gen4 was designed with concealed use in mind, although it still packs 13 rounds in its magazine.

BELOW: At just 6.41 inches (163mm) in length, the .40 G27 Gen4 offers the ultimate in pocket-sized firepower.

	GLOCK 23 Gen4	GLOCK 27 Gen4
CALIBER:	.40	.40
LENGTH:	7.28in (185mm)	6.41in (163mm)
HEIGHT:	4.99in (127mm)	4.17in (106mm)
WIDTH:	1.18in (30mm)	1.18in (30mm)
LENGTH BETWEEN SIGHTS:	6.02in (153mm)	5.39in (137mm)
BARREL HEIGHT:	1.26in (32mm)	1.26in (32mm)
BARREL LENGTH:	4.01in (102mm)	3.42in (87mm)
WEIGHT (UNLOADED):	23.65oz (670g)	21.89oz (620g)
WEIGHT (LOADED):	31.06oz (888g)	27.00oz (765g)
TRIGGER PULL:	~5.5lb (~2.5kg)	~5.5lb (~2.5kg)
TRIGGER TRAVEL:	~0.49in (~12.5mm)	~0.49in (~12.5mm)
BARREL RIFLING:	right hand, hexagonal	right hand, hexagonal
RIFLING LENGTH OF TWIST:	9.84in (250mm)	9.84in (250mm)
MAGAZINE CAPACITY (STANDARD):	13	9
MAGAZINE CAPACITY (OPTIONAL):	10/15/22	13/15/22

Glock 24 and 35

Glock's development of a .40-caliber needed a competition gun to round it
off, and the G24 seemed to be the answer. Introduced in 1994, the G24 was
basically the G17L in .40 caliber, with the standard .40 features such as an
extra locking-block pin. And yet, the G24 is the classic example of a sound
gun arriving at the wrong time. Patrick Sweeney explains in detail how,
at the moment the G24 arrived on the scene, the rest of the competition
world in the United States (the biggest market) had made a shift to very
different sorts of handgun for competition shooting, the vogue being for
high-capacity (25–28 rounds) .38 gun fitted with compensators and red-dot
sights. In this context, the Glock 24 looked a little stodgy and lacking the
paraphernalia that many shooters craved. Furthermore, the G24 wouldn't
actually fit within the IPSC regulation box, hence it was not allowed to be
used in a critical sector of the competition shooting field (Sweeney, 2008,
pp.146–47).

On account of these conditions, the G24 did not have a long life ahead
of it, especially as it was totally eclipsed by Glock's next .40 competition
model, the G35. This gun was released in January 1998, and it was a clear
competition gun in relation to the G22 on which it was based. Looking
at the Gen4 model (remember that the date of production meant that

BELOW: The G24C is the "compensated" version of the standard G24, meaning that the barrel is ported to direct muzzle gas upwards and therefore control muzzle flip.

the G35 went straight into Gen3 configuration), the differences between the G35 and standard G22 are striking. Whereas the G22 had an overall length of 8.03 inches (204mm), the competition G35 took the length up to 8.81 inches (224mm), with a 1.26-inch (135mm) barrel and a length between sights of 7.55 inches (192mm)—the latter dimension for the G22 is 6.49 inches (165mm), a marked difference. As with the G24, the G35 reduced its weight by milling open a slot on the top of the slide, this modification making it the same weight as the G22 slide. Nevertheless, the G35 is not a light gun, especially in terms of loaded weight. With a full 15-round standard magazine, the Glock 35 weighs 36.01 ounces (1,020g), breaking the 2.2-pound (1kg) mark, as opposed to the G22's loaded weight of 34.42 ounces (975g). This being said, the G35 had the lighter trigger pull of the Glock's competition guns, and combined with a heavier frame this makes the gun steady in the hand, a prerequisite of effective combat handgunning. Such has been proven in the G35's excellent performance in competitions to this day.

GLOCK 24C
DATE:
1990
CALIBER:
.40
LENGTH:
9.56in (243mm)
BARREL LENGTH:
6.02in (153mm)
WEIGHT (EMPTY):
26.75oz (758g)
MAGAZINE CAPACITY (STANDARD):
15
EFFECTIVE RANGE:
55yds (50m)

The 10mm Guns

The 10mm Auto cartridge has garnered a certain mystique about it, with dark rumors of its power circulating among the shooting community. Much of this mystique comes from its distinctive origins in the 1980s, courtesy of firearms legend Lieutenant Colonel John Dean "Jeff" Cooper. Cooper developed the cartridge in the early 1980s as an attempt to

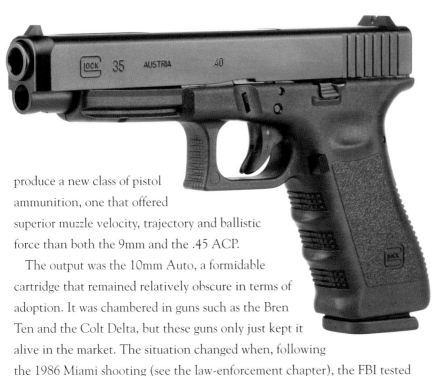

GLOCK 35
DATE: 1998
CALIBER: .40 Safe Action
LENGTH: 8.81in (224mm)
BARREL LENGTH: 5.31in (135mm)
WEIGHT (LOADED): 36.01oz (1,020g)
MAGAZINE CAPACITY (STANDARD): 15
RANGE: 50yds (45.72m)

produce a new class of pistol ammunition, one that offered superior muzzle velocity, trajectory and ballistic force than both the 9mm and the .45 ACP.

The output was the 10mm Auto, a formidable cartridge that remained relatively obscure in terms of adoption. It was chambered in guns such as the Bren Ten and the Colt Delta, but these guns only just kept it alive in the market. The situation changed when, following the 1986 Miami shooting (see the law-enforcement chapter), the FBI tested out the 10mm Auto as a possible replacement cartridge for a new bureau handgun. In the end they decided that the 10mm Auto was simply too powerful, creating the need for extended training

GLOCK 35 Gen4
DATE: 2010
CALIBER: .40
LENGTH: 8.74in (222mm)
BARREL LENGTH: 5.31in (135mm)
WEIGHT (LOADED): 36.18oz (1,025g)
MAGAZINE CAPACITY (STANDARD): 15
MAGAZINE CAPACITY (OPTIONAL): 10/22
EFFECTIVE RANGE: 50yds (45.72m)

RIGHT: The 10mm Auto cartridge is the most potent round that the Glock range can chamber, with impressive muzzle velocities of up to 1,400 feet per second (426 m/sec).

times. A reduced-recoil version was preferred, which in turn led to the creation of the .40 S&W cartridge.

As we have seen, the .40 cartridge took vigorous hold of the public imagination, and became a market-dominant cartridge for the 1990s and into the 21st century. However, the 10mm Auto stayed there in the background, garnering respect as the cartridge "too powerful for the FBI." Thus is was just a matter of time before the .40 emerged in a new series of guns, and that achievement came courtesy of Glock.

10mm Auto Performance

The 10mm Auto cartridge is undoubtedly a powerful performer. The bullet diameter is actually 0.4 inches (10.17mm), the case length being 0.99 inches (25.2mm) and the rim diameter 0.425 inches (10.8mm), and fitted with the Large Pistol primer. With some of the modern loadings, the 10mm Auto will deliver a 0.42 ounce (12g, 180-grain) bullet at 1,300 feet per second (396 m/sec) and a 0.31-ounce (8.7g, 135-grain) bullet at 1,400 feet per second (426 m/sec). Both these velocities exceed the best outputs of the .45 ACP using +P ammunition. Furthermore, the 10mm Auto also appears to be superior in terms of the energy delivery as well. Some of the most potent brands of 10mm Auto ammunition will generate 643 feet per pound (871 J) of energy, while the best that the .45 ACP will deliver is around 570 feet per pound (772 J). Although there is more to a cartridge than ballistic data, the specifications of the round indicate that it is a serious power option for a handgun.

FACING PAGE: A G20 on show at France's Milipol global security trade fair in Paris, 2009.

GLOCK 20
Cal. 10mm

GLOCK 20

DATE:
1990
CALIBER:
10mm Auto
LENGTH:
8.22in (209mm)
BARREL LENGTH:
4.6in (117mm)
WEIGHT (LOADED):
39.71oz (1,125g)
**MAGAZINE CAPACITY
(STANDARD):**
15
RANGE:
55yds (50m)

RIGHT: FBI agents train with the Glock. The FBI considered adopting the 10mm round as standard, but considered it too powerful.

Glock 20 and Glock 29

The Glock 20 is definitely one of the more muscular pistols in the Glock range. Launched in 1990 (and thus for a time quite overshadowed by the .40 guns), it packs 15 10mm Auto rounds into its magazine, only two less than the 9mm capacity of the standard G17. But to fit the sizeable cartridges in and cope with their recoil, Glock had to increase the frame size of the gun. This meant that the width crept up to 1.27 inches (32.5mm), while the depth of the grip swelled to accommodate the overall round length—1.260 inches (32mm) compared to the 1.169 inches (29.69mm) of the 9mm Parabellum.

What this means is that the Glock 20 is not entirely suitable for those with small hands, or who can't handle the combination of a beefy grip and a hefty recoil. This being said, field shooting reports of the Glock 20 are generally positive from those comfortable with handling big guns. The weight of the gun in its fully loaded condition is not exactly light—39.71 ounces (1,125g)—but then again the gun is still lighter than some other 10mm Auto handguns such as the Colt Delta Elite.

Glock was not dismissive of the needs of shooters with smaller hands, however, so it subsequently produced the Glock 20 SF. The "SF" suffix stands for "Short Frame," which in this case means that although the width of the gun stayed the same, the reach from the back of the grip to the trigger was reduced by 0.98 inches (2.5mm), with a reduction of the heel of the pistol by 0.16 inches (4mm). The overall gun dimensions remain the same, however. Note that the G20, as well as taking the full-power 10mm Auto, can also comfortably shoot the FBI's preferred lighter loading cartridges, making the firing experience a little gentler.

GLOCK 20C
DATE:
1990
CALIBER:
10mm Auto
LENGTH:
8.22in (209mm)
BARREL LENGTH:
4.6in (117mm)
WEIGHT (LOADED):
39.71oz (1,125g)
MAGAZINE CAPACITY (STANDARD):
15
RANGE:
55yds (50m)

	GLOCK 20 GEN4	GLOCK 29 GEN4
CALIBER:	10mm Auto	10mm Auto
LENGTH:	8.03in (204mm)	6.88in (175mm)
HEIGHT:	5.47in (139mm)	4.45in (113mm)
WIDTH:	1.27in (32.5mm)	1.27in (32.5mm)
LENGTH BETWEEN SIGHTS:	6.77in (172mm)	5.91in (150mm)
BARREL HEIGHT:	1.26in (32mm)	1.26in (32mm)
BARREL LENGTH:	4.6in (117mm)	3.77in (96mm)
WEIGHT (UNLOADED):	30.71oz (870g)	26.83oz (760g)
WEIGHT (LOADED):	39.54oz (1,120g)	32.65oz (925g)
TRIGGER PULL:	~5.5lb (~2.5kg)	~5.5lb (~2.5kg)
TRIGGER TRAVEL:	0.49in (~12.5mm)	0.49in (~12.5mm)
BARREL RIFLING:	right hand, hexagonal	right hand, hexagonal
RIFLING LENGTH OF TWIST:	9.84in (250mm)	9.84in (250mm)
MAGAZINE CAPACITY (STANDARD):	15	10
MAGAZINE CAPACITY (OPTIONAL):	n/a	15

GLOCK 29
DATE
1997
CALIBER:
10mm Auto
LENGTH:
6.96in (177mm)
BARREL LENGTH:
3.77in (96mm)
WEIGHT (LOADED):
33.01oz (935g)
MAGAZINE CAPACITY
(STANDARD):
10
RANGE:
50yds (45.72m)

The G29 option is another handgun in the 10mm range, and is certainty not for the timorous. The G29 is in the "subcompact" section of the Glock, which is quite adventurous considering the scale of the cartridge that it fires. The specifications speak for themselves. The Glock 20 Gen4, for example, has an overall length of 8.03 inches (204mm) and a barrel length of 4.6 inches (117mm). Those same statistics applied to the G29 are, respectively, 6.88 inches (175mm) and 3.77 inches (96mm), both dramatic shortenings.

The kick, noise, and blast from the gun are formidable and handling the weapon requires good training and muscle control. Nevertheless, for someone who wants to make an impression with a highly concealable handgun, the Glock 29 is good choice.

Glock 40

At the time of writing, the Glock 40 is one of the most recent additions to the Glock range, being launched in 2014. In basic layout, the gun connects naturally with its G20 forebear, but with all the benefits of the Gen4 configuration. Given the power of the cartridge the gun is firing, the dual recoil-spring system fitted inside is appreciated, not only for its recoil-mollifying properties but also for the greater system durability it appears to provide.

The Glock 40 is certainly a sizeable gun, following in the clear tradition of the 10mm Auto pistols. The Glock website refers to the handgun as a "Long Slide" weapon, and the slide certainly is that—the overall length of the gun is 9.49 inches (241mm), giving a length between sights of 8.19 inches (208mm). Magazine capacity as standard is 15 rounds. One interesting point made visible on the company website is the fact that the G40's magazines have been produced to drop clear of the gun when the magazine release button is pressed.

GLOCK 29 SF
DATE:
2009
CALIBER:
10mm Auto
LENGTH:
6.88in (175mm)
BARREL LENGTH:
3.77in (96mm)
WEIGHT (LOADED):
32.65oz (925g)
MAGAZINE CAPACITY
(STANDARD):
10
RANGE:
50yds (45.72m)

GLOCK 40 GEN4

DATE:
2015
CALIBER:
10mm Auto
LENGTH:
9.49in (241mm)
BARREL LENGTH:
6.02in (153mm)
WEIGHT (LOADED):
40.14oz (1,138g)
MAGAZINE CAPACITY (STANDARD):
15
EFFECTIVE RANGE:
50yds (45.72m)

Yet one of the real distinguishing features of the Glock 40 is that instead of the standard rear-sight notch the top of the slide is fitted with a modular mounting plate, which can take a variety of sight fittings. Glock is promoting the gun (along with the G34, G35, and G41) in the Modular Optic System (MOS) configuration. What the MOS achieves is to give a simple and easily adapted mounting system for the miniature electro-optical reflex sights that have become available for handgunners wanting a bit more precision behind their shooting. Reflex sights work by placing a colored dot of light onto the aiming point, the dot size typically covering three minutes of angle (MOA) or, for a larger sight picture, seven MOA. Note that with traditional iron sights, the shooter must align three objects: the rear sight, the front sight and the target, but with a reflex sight the burden is reduced by allowing the shooter purely to concentrate on the target, while maneuvering the illuminated dot to fall upon the target. Reflex sights offer several advantages compared to regular iron sights. First, they give quick target

RIGHT: This Glock 40 Gen4 includes the Modular Optic System (MOS) sight.

acquisition—all the shooter has to do is keep both eyes open and on the target and bring up the sight quickly to place the colored dot on the aiming point. Also, the reflex sight can be a useful aid to accurate long-distance shooting, as any wavering off target is more easily perceived.

What Glock provides with the MOS is a mounting plate that can be fitted securely to the rear of the slide, and which then takes one of four adapter plates to grip the optical sight. The system is extremely robust—it has to be, as the sight must go through the brutal forces of recoil and slide return without being shaken off its mount or losing its accuracy.

The Glock .40 and 10mm models are serious power players in the world of combat handguns. As we will see in the chapter on law-enforcement use of the Glock, these calibers have been subject to the forces of fashion, and also to a new emerging realism about what truly constitutes a practical caliber for self-defense. But as we have seen with the MOS guns, Glock is continually offering mechanisms by which its range of calibers can be delivered onto the target with more accuracy. We shall see the same attitude at work in our next chapter.

ABOVE: This target shooter is using a G40 fitted with the Modular Optic System (MOS), a new optical sighting option from Glock.

The .45, .380, and .357 Glocks

When it comes to the matter of handgun caliber, there is something of a distinction between the European and the Americans. In Europe, the 9mm cartridge has held sway above all others, and it shows no sign of losing its top position. Americans also use the 9mm in large numbers—it is the most popular overall caliber—but there is also a love affair in the country with the big old .45 cartridge, as established by the Colt M1911.

FACING PAGE: Actor Sylvester Stallone wields a .45-caliber Glock 21 during the movie *Escape Plan* (2013).

The .45 ACP is undeniably an excellent combat cartridge. The substantial mass of the bullet, usually 0.42–0.53 ounces (12–15g, 185–230 grain), its broad caliber, and muzzle velocities in the region of 984 feet per second (300 m/sec) deliver accuracy, deep penetration, and a severe permanent cavitation in those unlucky enough to be struck by the round. (The penetration depth for some of the advanced modern cartridges can be as high as 26 inches [686mm].) The major downside, however, is that .45 handguns, even with double-stack magazine ingenuity, tend to have an ammo capacity significantly below that of guns in 9mm and .40 caliber. For this reason, the .45 ACP has largely played second fiddle in terms of volume sales in comparison with these smaller calibers. Yet the .45 ACP endures, and continues to be adopted by police officers, military units, and defense-minded civilians.

BELOW: The .45 ACP cartridge has served military and law-enforcement customers well since the early 1900s.

RIGHT: Glock handguns, such as this G21, display the model and the caliber on the gun slide, plus the serial number and country of origin.

Glock 21

For Glock it would have been commercially unwise to ignore this reality, and in December 1991 it unveiled its first .45 ACP handguns—the Glock 21. In terms of designing a weapon to handle the big cartridge, this wasn't too much of a leap for Glock, as it had already produced the 10mm G20. Indeed, the G21 was in dimensional terms the same as the G20, and presented the identical challenge for the small-handed user. Like the G20, however, the G21 has also been produced in a short-frame version, the G21 SF, to adapt to those who need a shorter grip. In the Gen4 version of the G21, the MBS design also lets the shooter make some dimensional

	GLOCK 21	GLOCK 21 SF
CALIBER:	.45 Auto	.45 Auto
LENGTH:	8.22in (209mm)	8.03in (204mm)
HEIGHT:	5.47in (139mm)	5.47in (139mm)
WIDTH:	1.27in (32.5mm)	1.27in (32.5mm)
LENGTH BETWEEN SIGHTS:	6.77in (172mm)	6.77in (172mm)
BARREL HEIGHT:	1.26in (32mm)	1.26in (32mm)
BARREL LENGTH:	4.6in (117mm)	4.6in (117mm)
WEIGHT (UNLOADED):	29.84oz (835g)	29.3oz (830g)
WEIGHT (LOADED):	38.48oz (1,090g)	38.3oz (1,085g)
TRIGGER PULL:	~5.5lb (~2.5kg)	~5.5lb (~2.5kg)
TRIGGER TRAVEL:	0.49in (~12.5mm)	0.49in (~12.5mm)
BARREL RIFLING:	right hand, hexagonal	right hand, hexagonal
RIFLING LENGTH OF TWIST:	15.75in (400mm)	15.75in (400mm)
MAGAZINE CAPACITY (STANDARD):	13	13
MAGAZINE CAPACITY (OPTIONAL):	10	10

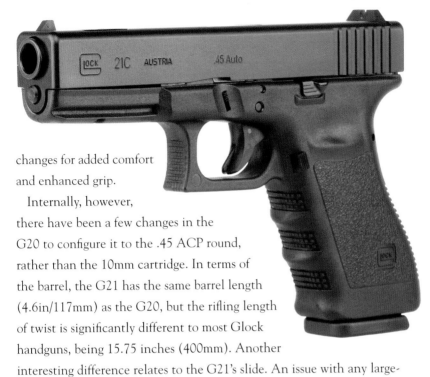

GLOCK 21C
DATE:
2007
CALIBER:
.45 Auto
LENGTH:
8.22in (209mm)
BARREL LENGTH:
4.6in (117mm)
WEIGHT (LOADED):
38.48oz (1,090g)
MAGAZINE CAPACITY
(STANDARD):
13
RANGE:
50yds (45.72m)

changes for added comfort and enhanced grip.

Internally, however, there have been a few changes in the G20 to configure it to the .45 ACP round, rather than the 10mm cartridge. In terms of the barrel, the G21 has the same barrel length (4.6in/117mm) as the G20, but the rifling length of twist is significantly different to most Glock handguns, being 15.75 inches (400mm). Another interesting difference relates to the G21's slide. An issue with any large-caliber handgun is keeping down the weight. We have already seen a solution to this problem in several Glock models—cutting away a portion of the upper slide to reduce the weight of metal. In the G21, however, we see a different solution.

Here the slide itself is thinned along the sides, in front of the ejection port, making a total weight saving of 1.4 ounces (40g). This brings the total empty weight of the G21 Gen4 down to 29.3 ounces (830g), compared to the 30.89 ounces (875g) for the G20. The G21's loaded weight is also below that the G20—38.3 ounces (1,085g) vs. 39.71 ounces (1,125g)—but here we have to acknowledge that the G21 has a magazine holding 13 rounds as standard, rather than the 15 rounds offered by the G20. Like the G20, the G21 also has the option of 10-round magazines if desired.

The G21 has performed generally well in the hands of gun reviewers. Some have noted that because the overall structure of the gun was designed for the more powerful 10mm round, the G21 can have cycling problems if it is loaded with light load cartridges, rather than full-power cartridges, especially if the operator holds the gun with a weak grip that doesn't give the slide operation enough resistance. The easy solution is to load up the G21 with good +P ammo; giving the gun some extra boost is not likely to be a problem for a shooter who wanted a powerful handgun in the first place.

RIGHT: Introduced in 1996, the G30 (here seen in its Gen4 configuration) holds 11 rounds of .45 ACP.

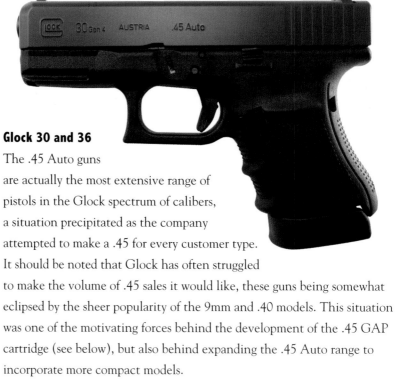

Glock 30 and 36

The .45 Auto guns are actually the most extensive range of pistols in the Glock spectrum of calibers, a situation precipitated as the company attempted to make a .45 for every customer type. It should be noted that Glock has often struggled to make the volume of .45 sales it would like, these guns being somewhat eclipsed by the sheer popularity of the 9mm and .40 models. This situation was one of the motivating forces behind the development of the .45 GAP cartridge (see below), but also behind expanding the .45 Auto range to incorporate more compact models.

The G30 was produced from 1996, and was a subcompact version of the G21. As with all Glock subcompacts, the dimensions of the weapon had

GLOCK 36
DATE:
1999
CALIBER:
.45
LENGTH:
6.96in (177mm)
BARREL LENGTH:
3.77in (96mm)
WEIGHT (EMPTY):
22.42oz (635g)
MAGAZINE CAPACITY
(STANDARD):
6
EFFECTIVE RANGE:
40yds (37m)

	GLOCK 30 GEN4	GLOCK 36
CALIBER:	.45 Auto	.45 Auto
LENGTH:	6.88in (175mm)	6.96in (177mm)
HEIGHT:	4.80in (122mm)	4.76in (121mm)
WIDTH:	1.27in (32.5mm)	1.13in (28.7mm)
LENGTH BETWEEN SIGHTS:	5.91in (150mm)	5.91in (150mm)
BARREL HEIGHT:	1.26in (32mm)	1.26in (32mm)
BARREL LENGTH:	3.77in (96mm)	3.77in (96mm)
WEIGHT (UNLOADED):	26.3oz (745g)	22.42oz (635g)
WEIGHT (LOADED):	33.71oz (955g)	27oz (765g)
TRIGGER PULL:	~5.5lb (~2.5kg)	~5.5lb (~2.5kg)
TRIGGER TRAVEL:	0.49in (~12.5mm)	0.49in (~12.5mm)
BARREL RIFLING:	right hand, octagonal	right hand, octagonal
RIFLING LENGTH OF TWIST:	15.75in (400mm)	15.75in (400mm)
MAGAZINE CAPACITY (STANDARD):	10	6
MAGAZINE CAPACITY (OPTIONAL):	13	–

dropped appreciably. The width of the gun remained the same, hence it still had a chunky grip, but the overall length had descended to 6.96 inches (177mm) and a barrel length of 3.77 inches (96mm), with a length between sights of 5.91 inches (150mm). In the Gen4 model, the overall length went down further, to 6.88 inches (175mm), although the two other dimensions given for the standard G30 remained the same. The weight of the gun also went down appreciably—26.48 ounces (750g) empty, and 33.89 ounces (960g) loaded.

Like all Glock subcompact guns, the G30 requires that the user modifies his grip significantly, usually with the little finger hooked beneath the magazine base plate. The shooter also has to be more conservative with ammo expenditure—the G30 holds just 10 rounds as standard, although the G21 13-round magazines can be used as well.

The G30 is a solid proposition if the purchaser wants a hard-hitting gun, but one that can be transported with ease of concealment. Although the reduction in the barrel length shaves off around 50 feet per second (15m/sec) from the muzzle velocity, for close-quarters self-defense purposes this isn't really significant, and the bullet will still leave the barrel at around 775 feet per second (236 m/sec) and carry enough energy to do its damage to an assailant.

FACING PAGE: A range officer supervises a citizen police academy member in handling a Glock at a police firing range, Colorado.

In itself the G30 is the basis of its own mini range of Glock guns. In addition to the G30 Gen4, there is also the G30 SF, for those wanting the gun in a short-frame format. A more interesting addition is the G30S. Here we have the G30 SF frame, but the lower part of the gun is fitted with a slimmer slide, to make the gun both lighter and more easily concealed. The total unloaded weight of the gun is 22.95 ounces (650g), and once loaded with 10 rounds of .45 ACP this climbs up to 30.36 ounces (860g).

But beyond the G30 SF and G30S, there is an even lighter option for the shooter who wants to pack a .45 Glock. This is the G36, a "subcompact slimline" model that goes to the limits of frame size for the .45 cartridge, with the slide reduced down to 1.13 inches (28.7mm). The G36 is only a six-round gun, however, although it can take magazines with custom extension baseplates to add one or two rounds to the gun. (The extension can also make the Glock's short handle slightly easier to grip.)

GLOCK 30S
DATE:
2013
CALIBER:
.45 Auto
LENGTH:
6.96in (177mm)
BARREL LENGTH:
3.77in (96mm)
WEIGHT (LOADED):
30.36oz (860g)
MAGAZINE CAPACITY (STANDARD):
10
EFFECTIVE RANGE:
50yds (45.72m)

GLOCK 30 SF
DATE:
2010
CALIBER:
.45 Auto
LENGTH:
6.88in (175mm)
BARREL LENGTH:
3.77in (96mm)
WEIGHT (LOADED):
33.7oz (955g)
MAGAZINE CAPACITY (STANDARD):
10
EFFECTIVE RANGE:
50yds (45.72m)

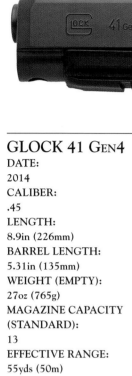

GLOCK 41 Gen4
DATE:
2014
CALIBER:
.45
LENGTH:
8.9in (226mm)
BARREL LENGTH:
5.31in (135mm)
WEIGHT (EMPTY):
27oz (765g)
MAGAZINE CAPACITY
(STANDARD):
13
EFFECTIVE RANGE:
55yds (50m)

Glock 41

But the G30S is not the end of the Glock .45 range. Released at the beginning of 2015, the G41 Gen4 has just arrived on the scene, offering the very latest in advanced Glock technology. The G41 is at the opposite end of the scale from the G36 in terms of size. Designed from the outset as a tactical or competition handgun, the G41 is a sizeable piece—the total length of the gun is 8.9 inches (226mm), with a barrel measuring no less than 5.31 inches (135mm). These dimension result in a long sight radius of 7.56 inches (192mm), making accurate shots above the typical 55-yard (50 m) maximum range of most handguns perfectly feasible. Indeed, in some accuracy tests shooters armed with the G41 have hit small steel plates at distances in excess of 200 yards (183m). The accuracy of the gun is helped by the adjustable rear notch sight, which, with the aid of a screwdriver, can be adjusted for both windage and elevation. If the shooter chooses, the gun can also be provided in the MOS configuration, to take combat optics at the rear of the slide.

The noticeably longer slide on the G41 does not mean that the gun becomes excessively heavy. In fact, the G41's slide is specially thinned down to control the weight of such a large gun; the loaded weight, with a full 13-round magazine, is 36 ounces (1,020g), 27 ounces (765g) being the gun itself minus the ammunition. In fact, despite being one of the larger Glock guns the G41 actually weighs 2.3 ounces (65g) lighter than the lightest of the three other full-size .45s: G21, G21 Gen4, and G21 SF.

The author has not fired one of the new Glocks, but press reports seem generally favorable. On account of the longer barrel, the gun sends out its rounds at a brisk muzzle velocity of between 800 feet per second (243 m/sec) and 1,000 feet per second (305 m/sec), depending on the weight of the rounds. Accuracy reports are also confidence-building, with admittedly experienced hands producing 0.5-inch (12.7mm) groups at 25 yards (23m). Recoil control is aided by the lengthier slide plus the Gen4's double-spring recoil system.

The .45 GAP Glocks

The .45 GAP—Glock Auto Pistol—is one of the most interesting developments in the recent history of handgun ammunition development. The .45 ACP was, and is, a powerful and practical cartridge, of that there is no argument. Yet Glock realized that the dimensions of the cartridge were something of a burden, compelling the guns that took the round to be bulky compared to the 9mm and .40-caliber models, the two types that were selling especially well during the 1990s and early 2000s. So, Glock tasked expert Ernest Durham, of the CCI/Speed company, with a challenge—produce a .45-caliber round but in a shortened

GLOCK 41 GEN4 MOS
DATE:
2014
CALIBER:
.45
LENGTH:
8.9in (226mm)
BARREL LENGTH:
5.31in (135mm)
WEIGHT (EMPTY):
27oz (765g)
MAGAZINE CAPACITY (STANDARD):
13
EFFECTIVE RANGE:
55yds (50m)

ABOVE: Sherriff's deputies from Onondaga, New York, practice with their .45-caliber Glocks during range training.

FACING PAGE: Actor R. Lee Ermey attends an event promoting Team Glock. A former US Marine, Ermey is best known for his role as Gunnery Sergeant Hartman in the 1987 movie *Full Metal Jacket*. Ermey has since become an official spokesperson for Glock firearms in the United States.

format that would fit the dimensions of the G17/G22 platform. Oh, and while he was at it, the new cartridge had to deliver the same ballistic performance as the old .45 ACP.

In late 2002, the new cartridge was approved as the .45 GAP, the first Glock cartridge specifically branded with the company name. The case length was just 0.755 inches (19.2mm), which was actually shorter than the 0.754 inches (19.15mm) of the 9mm Parabellum. The bullet weight sat at 0.46 ouches (13 g, 200 grains), which fell a little short of the 0.53 ounces (15g, 230 grains) of the full-weight .45 ACP cartridge, although the muzzle velocity and energy were not far off the original model. However, within a short space of time the ammunition engineers were able to upgrade the cartridge to fire the 0.53-ounce (15g, 230-grain) bullet at just the same performance levels as the .45 ACP. This was an impressive feat, considering that the ballistics of the .45 GAP were dependent upon the propellant loading alone, within a much shorter cartridge case.

GLOCK 37
DATE:
2004
CALIBER:
.45 GAP
LENGTH:
8.03in (204mm)
BARREL LENGTH:
4.48in (114mm)
WEIGHT (LOADED):
35.48oz (1,005g)
MAGAZINE CAPACITY (STANDARD):
10
EFFECTIVE RANGE:
50yds (45.72m)

Having produced this ingenious cartridge, Glock then had to deliver the guns to match. The baseline design was the G37, which Glock officially advocates as "our answer to big bore muzzle flip and high velocity recoil." The G37 almost exactly squares up in terms of dimensions with the .40 G22. However, the .45 GAP handgun has received some significant re-engineering to take the new round and handle its power. Not only is there a different barrel, with a 15.75-inch (400mm) length of twist as opposed to the 9.84-inch (250mm) twist of the G22, but the slide is also a more substantial affair, to cope with the extra recoil drive of the larger round. In fact, the G37 slide is actually 25 percent heavier than that of the G22, and a full 33 percent heavier than the G17 slide. Sweeney notes that "The unlocking mass (combined weight of the barrel and slide) for the G-38 is 12 percent higher than that of the 1911, an impressive difference when you consider the fact that the barrel of the G-37 is half an inch shorter

GLOCK 38
DATE:
2005
CALIBER:
.45 GAP
LENGTH:
7.36in (187mm)
BARREL LENGTH:
4.01in (102mm)
WEIGHT (LOADED):
31.95oz (905g)
MAGAZINE CAPACITY
(STANDARD):
8
EFFECTIVE RANGE:
50yds (45.72m)

than that of the government Model 1911" (Sweeney, 2008, p.185). So while the loaded weight of the G22 is 34.42 ounces (975 kg), that of the G37 is 35.48 ounces (1,005g), a significant increase.

The G37, in its Gen4 format, has seen not only good civilian sales, but also adoption by some high-profile police forces, including the New York State Police and the Florida Highway Patrol. In customary fashion, Glock has also expanded the range to include a compact (G38) and a subcompact (G39) version. The format and design of these two guns reflects those of other .45 compact and subcompact Glocks, so will not be repeated in detail here. Suffice to note that the G38 will take 10-round magazines as standard, while for the G39 the standard capacity is just six rounds, with the option for a 10-round magazine that extends below the base of the grip.

GLOCK 39
DATE:
2004
CALIBER:
.45 GAP
LENGTH:
6.49in (165mm)
BARREL LENGTH:
3.42in (87mm)
WEIGHT (LOADED):
28.24oz (800g)
MAGAZINE CAPACITY
(STANDARD):
6
RANGE:
40yds (36.5m)

	.357 MAGNUM CARTRIDGE
CASE TYPE:	Rimmed
BULLET DIAMETER:	0.357in (9.1mm)
NECK DIAMETER:	0.379in (9.6mm)
BASE DIAMETER:	0.379in (9.6mm)
RIM DIAMETER:	0.440in (11.2mm)
RIM THICKNESS	0.06in (1.5mm)
CASE LENGTH:	1.29in (33mm)
OVERALL LENGTH:	1.59in (40mm)
PRIMER TYPE:	Small pistol, magnum
MAXIMUM PRESSURE:	35,000psi (241 MPa)

The .357 Glocks

Among handgun enthusiasts of the 1990s, one cartridge had a power status that was just as hallowed as that of the .45 ACP—the .357 Magnum. The problem was that this cartridge was only designed for use in high-power revolvers; it was simply too long to be adapted easily for auto pistol use, although some did try. What was needed—rather like the .45 GAP situation described above—was a cartridge that delivered the same ballistic performance as the Magnum round, but in a reduced size suitable for stacking in a box magazine.

It was the engineers at SIGARMS who came up with the solution, the .357 SIG. (It should be noted in passing that Glock rarely uses the name of the cartridge originator in its designations. Hence you will see references to .40 and .357 Glocks, but not to .40 S&W and .357 SIG Glocks.) What the SIG engineers did was to take a .40 S&W case, already a powerful round, and up the performance by necking it down to 0.355 inches (9mm), while also very slightly increasing the overall case length.

BELOW: The .357 Magnum cartridge, one of the most potent revolver cartridges in use.

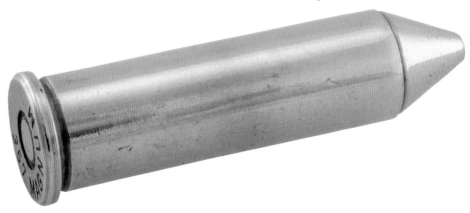

So what did SIG end up with regarding performance? Bear in mind that the .357 Magnum can throw out a 8.1g (125-grain) bullet at 442m/sec (1450ft/sec). In comparison, some of the modern .357 SIG loadings, such as the Federal Premium JHP, can fire the same 0.29-ounce (8.1g, 125-grain) bullet at 1,436 feet per second (436 m/sec). Yet whereas the .357 Magnum had a case length of 1.29 inches (33mm), the .357 SIG case length was just 0.865 inches (21.97mm). As with the development of the .45 GAP, the .357 SIG demonstrated the ingenuity of those who really understood their physics.

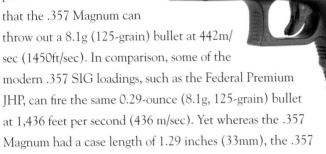

The first gun to emerge from Glock for the new round was the G31 in August 1996. The G31 was in essence a G22 but rebarelled for the .357-caliber round, resulting in the same dimensions but with fractionally different weights. In fact, those with a G22 can convert it to the G31 basically by buying and installing a different barrel; even the magazines don't need to change.

What the G31 offered was the power of the .357 Magnum but without the wrist-snapping handling characteristics of the revolver cartridge. Glock has produced around this cartridge three core guns and their Gen4 derivatives. Predictably enough, the three core guns are the standard (G31), compact (G32), and subcompact (G33), each having its own Gen4 model.

The recoil and blast from the potent .357 cartridge crank up in the smaller models, while the magazine capacity declines. With the G32, for example, the barrel length drops down to 4.01 inches (102mm) and the standard mag capacity is 13 rounds, while in the G33 the barrel goes down to just 3.42 inches (87mm), and the standard magazine to nine rounds, albeit with options for 13- or 15-round mags. The .357 round emerging from such a short barrel, and anchored by a short grip, is not for everyone, but as personal defense weapons for those with the handling experience, the G32 and G33 can do the job.

GLOCK 31
DATE:
1998
CALIBER:
.357
LENGTH:
8.03in (204mm)
BARREL LENGTH:
4.48in (114mm)
WEIGHT (LOADED):
33.18oz (940g)
MAGAZINE CAPACITY (STANDARD):
15
EFFECTIVE RANGE:
50yds (45.72m)

LEFT: The G31C, or "compensated" model of the G31.

GLOCK 32
DATE:
1998
CALIBER:
.357 Safe Action
LENGTH:
7.36in (187mm)
BARREL LENGTH:
4.01in (102mm)
WEIGHT (LOADED):
31.18oz (855g)
MAGAZINE CAPACITY
(STANDARD):
13
EFFECTIVE RANGE:
50yds (45.72m)

RIGHT: The G32C is the
compensated version of
the standard G32.

GLOCK 33
DATE:
1998
CALIBER:
.357 Safe Action
LENGTH:
6.49in (165mm)
BARREL LENGTH:
3.42in (87mm)
WEIGHT (LOADED):
26.65oz (755g)
MAGAZINE CAPACITY
(STANDARD):
9
EFFECTIVE RANGE:
50yds (45.72m)

The .380 Auto Glocks

The .380 Auto (9 x 17mm) cartridge is something of a curious case in the history of handgun ammunition. What makes it interesting is that, in many ways, the cartridge is rather poor for the self-defense purposes to which it has been put. Developed in 1908 by none other than John Browning, the .380 Auto is a very low-powered cartridge, with comparatively poor velocity and ballistic force. By way of comparison, 9mm Parabellum JHP ammunition, fired from a 4.65-inch (118mm) barrel, sends out a 0.26-ounce (7.45g, 115-grain) bullet at 1,397 feet per second (426 m/sec), and thereby delivers 500 feet per pound (678 J) to the target. Now square that up against the .380 Auto, which also (in metric) has a 9mm caliber. Admittedly fired from a shorter barrel—3.75in (950mm)—a diminutive 0.21-ounce (6g, 90-grain) round leaves the muzzle at just 984 feet per second (300 m/sec) and packs 200 feet per pound (270 J) of energy.

Note that such lackluster performance has put gunmakers off making handguns in the caliber, or buyers purchasing such weapons. Famous guns in this caliber include some varieties of the Walther PP range plus the Beretta 1934. But looked at objectively the .380 Auto does offer some advantages. The power may be low but so is the recoil, making it a fitting handgun for someone with little time to invest in training. The limited force of the cartridge is also such that it can be used in straightforward blowback guns, which don't require a locking mechanism to restrain a more powerful cartridge type. Consequently, .380 Auto guns can have fixed barrels, and this makes them very accurate, at least within the limits of the cartridge range (up to 55 yards/50m). The guns for this cartridge can also reach ultra-compact dimensions, ideal for concealed back-up guns, suitable to slip into a small bag or pocket. Furthermore, in self-defense terms it is arguably better to have any sort of gun rather than no gun at all, hence even the .380 Auto has a market. It should also be accepted that just as the power of other cartridge types has been improved through development of propellant load characteristics, so too has the .380 Auto benefitted from such changes.

GLOCK 28

DATE:
1997
CALIBER:
.380 Auto
LENGTH:
6.49in (165mm)
BARREL LENGTH:
3.42 in (87mm)
WEIGHT (LOADED):
23.83oz (675g)
MAGAZINE CAPACITY (STANDARD):
10
EFFECTIVE RANGE:
50yds (45.72m)

	GLOCK 25	GLOCK 42
CALIBER:	.380 Auto	.380 Auto
LENGTH:	7.36in (187mm)	5.94in (151mm)
HEIGHT:	4.99in (127mm)	4.13in (105mm)
WIDTH:	1.18in (30mm)	0.94in (24mm)
LENGTH BETWEEN SIGHTS:	6.02in (153mm)	4.92in (125mm)
BARREL HEIGHT:	1.26in (32mm)	n/a
BARREL LENGTH:	4.01in (102mm)	3.25in (82.5mm)
WEIGHT (UNLOADED):	23.3oz (640g)	13.76oz (390g)
WEIGHT (LOADED):	31.7oz (775g)	17.29oz (490g)
TRIGGER PULL:	~5.5lb (~2.5kg)	~5.5lb (~2.5kg)
TRIGGER TRAVEL:	0.49in (~12.5mm)	0.49in (~12.5mm)
BARREL RIFLING:	right hand, hexagonal	right hand, hexagonal
RIFLING LENGTH OF TWIST:	9.84in (250mm)	9.84in (250mm)
MAGAZINE CAPACITY (STANDARD):	15	6

Glock has recognized this fact with three particular .380 Auto models—the G25, G28 and, most recently, the G42. The G25 was actually produced mainly for civilian buyers in countries that prohibited the same of larger calibers to non-service personnel. Furthermore, because of various legalities regarding operating mechanisms in the United States the G25, and its compact derivative, the G28, are only available to law-enforcement officers, doubtless as a convenient back-up gun to complement their standard firearm.

What makes the G25 and G28 distinctive is that they are actually straight blowback guns, the power of the case recoil driving back an unlocked slide. However, they still have a hinged barrel like the standard guns, not a fixed variety, the barrel dropping down during the recoil to allow full slide cycling. Essentially what you have in the G25 is a blowback version of the G19, while the G28 mirrors the dimensions of the G26. The G25 can take an appreciable 15 rounds in its magazine, while with the G28 the capacity falls to 10 rounds. The overall height of the G28 is just 4.17 inches (106mm), and the other dimensions reflect the fact that this is a seriously compact firearm—a total length of 6.41 inches (165mm), a barrel length of 3.42 inches (87mm) and a total loaded weight of 23.83 ounces (675g).

BELOW: The G25 has been described by Glock as the "mild-mannered Glock," by virtue of its comfortable recoil.

Yet the G28 has now been rather surpassed in terms of handgun compression by the new G42, released in 2015. To make the .380-caliber available to its civilian customers, Glock has produced the G28 in the classic locked-breech system used by most of the other Glock guns. It has also made several other adaptations, on account of the pistol's dimensions. First, to ensure that the G28 fits as comfortably as possible in the hand, the backstrap extends further down until it is almost flush with the magazine baseplate, meaning that the back of the hand has more grip surface. Note also that even though the G42 has emerged so recently, it does not incorporate the MBS feature seen on the Gen4 guns. Mechanically, some adjustments have also been made to the firing pin safety, the slide stop lever coil spring, and the trigger return spring, to ensure the Glock levels of performance within the small frame.

The G42 is a straight-up Glock, immediately recognizable as one of the family and handling in the same manner. What is striking, however, is just what a lot of gun Glock have managed to drop into a hand-sized package. Consider some of the key dimensions here. A barrel measuring just 3.25 inches (82.5mm) in a gun that, from muzzle to the heel of the grip is only 5.94 inches (151mm). Height is 4.13 inches (105mm), which means that the G42 can only take six of the .380 Auto rounds, although the shooter can drop one into the chamber when the gun is first loaded, to give it a 6 + 1 capacity. Glock provides official details on the power of the weapon: with a typical load the G42 fires a 0.21-ounce (6g, 95-grain) bullet at 1,000 feet per second (328 m/sec) with 200 feet per pound (270 J).

The G42 is the polar opposite to the big 10mm or .45 Auto Glocks we have seen elsewhere in this chapter. And yet what it demonstrates is the intrinsic quality and functionality of the basic Glock design, such that it can easily be repurposed for almost every popular round in handgunning.

LEFT: The .380 G42 delivers a 95-grain (6g) bullet at around 1,000 feet per second (328m/sec).

ABOVE: This G42 magazine is fitted with an extension, which replaces the baseplate and provides an additional grip surface.

Handling the Glock

Handling the Glock is, in many ways, the same as handling any other type of semi-automatic handgun. For this reason some of the techniques of loading, firing, grip, and troubleshooting in this chapter will have a generic feel to them. Yet it is important that these are reiterated, even for those individuals who are seasoned in handling firearms in general. Every year, hundreds of people are killed in firearms accidents, and many of them have been shooting and maintaining guns for much of their lives. Do remember, it only takes a single lapse in safety to produce a fatality, so be ultra-vigilant for yourself and for others whenever a gun rests in your hand.

FACING PAGE: Tori Nonaka of Team Glock shows a perfectly balanced posture while delivering controlled fire onto a target.

Fundamental Rules of Gun Safety

1) **Treat any gun as loaded**—When you handle the Glock, regard it as a loaded weapon until you categorically verify otherwise. Inspect the grip to see if a magazine is in place, and if it is then eject it to see whether it has rounds stacked up or if it is empty. Also pull back the slide and inspect the chamber thoroughly, both visually and also physically, by slipping a digit into the end of the chamber. By performing these checks you can ensure that the gun is completely safe for handling.

2) **Muzzle control**—Muzzle control should follow the rule of the two "Cs": Constant and Conscious. By "Constant," I mean that the muzzle should be pointing in a safe direction at all times, regardless of whether you think the gun is safe or not. The old adage applies—never point a gun at anything that you are not prepared to destroy. Following on from this

RIGHT: A shooter makes a visual inspection of his Glock to ensure that no cartridges are in the chamber.

principle is the "Conscious" aspect. Keep your attention on the gun, and don't let your mind and your muzzle drift when thinking about other things.

3) **Finger off the trigger**—The Glock is an extremely safe gun to use, on account of its three-safety system. Nevertheless, if a cartridge is in the chamber and you pull the trigger, the gun will fire. For this reason, don't put your finger on the trigger unless your are consciously about to shoot. At all other times, keep your index finger resting beneath the trigger guard or pointing forward and touching the front of the trigger guard. Also be aware of anything that the trigger might snag on, producing an accidental discharge. This is a particular danger when holstering or otherwise storing the gun; keep your finger well away from the trigger when holstering, and inspect holsters and clothing for any projections that might snag the trigger.

LEFT: For patently obvious reasons, keep your finger well clear of the trigger when holstering or unholstering a Glock.

4) **Target awareness**—The effective range of a handgun is usually in the region of about 55 yards (50m), but its lethality will extend to many hundreds of yards. When you square up to a target, ask yourself the question: "If I miss, or the bullet passes straight through, what will it hit?" You should have a clear answer to this question before you start to send rounds downrange. Never discharge the gun at a target that doesn't have an inert physical backstop of some description, such as an earth bank, and also use your peripheral vision to check that people or other living creatures aren't moving progressively into your line of sight.

Training Glocks

Before launching into a discussion of the principles of handling real Glocks, some mention of Glock's several training models is required. Developing a range of non-firing training models is a judicious move, given the scale of Glock sales to military and law-enforcement organizations. The training phase of any handgun instruction course is the most dangerous of all, as an instructor will have to keep an eye on multiple people at any one time, many of whom won't have the fundamentals of gun safety built into their muscle memory. What the training models provide, therefore, is a safe way

RIGHT: 9mm cases fly from a G17, here fitted with an extended magaine. The slide is at the rear of its recoil phase.

for all present to handle the Glock in an authentic way, but without the danger. Furthermore, some guns in the series, as we shall see, also assist in the instruction of realistic tactical techniques, through firing non-lethal ammunition. One further point—in most cases the training Glocks are only sold to law-enforcement organizations through official channels. This is because the guns are far from toys. The training models are bona fide Glocks, including official Glock serial numbers. Most importantly, some of the guns can be converted to live-fire by swapping out parts, hence Glock is keen to keep a tight control over their distribution.

GLOCK 22 CUT

DATE:
1990
CALIBER:
n/a
LENGTH:
8.03in (204mm)
BARREL LENGTH:
4.49in (114mm)
WEIGHT (LOADED):
34.42oz (975g)
**MAGAZINE CAPACITY
(STANDARD):**
15
EFFECTIVE RANGE:
50yds (45.72m)

The first of the Glock training models to mention is the G22 Cut. The "Cut" stands for "Cutaway," referring to the fact that sections of the slide and frame are cut away to expose the inner workings of the gun, such as the barrel, chamber, locking block, recoil spring, and magazine spring. Cutaway guns are intended to be used for providing instruction to firearm technicians and also to Glock handlers who need to get familiar with the internals of the weapon. At the time of writing, the cutaway guns are: Gen3: G17, G19, G20, G21, G22, and G23; Gen4: G17.

For more interactive training models, the G17 P and G22 P are options. The "P" stands for "practice," and that's just what these guns are for. In every aspect, except the ability to fire, the P models are identical to their firing G17 and G22 counterparts. What this means is that trainees can handle a gun that looks, feels, loads, aims, and strips like a regular Glock, giving them invaluable but safe experience before they venture out onto the live guns. Yet because of the authenticity of the weapons, Glock has been extra careful to ensure that they can't be confused with the firing versions. The entire frame of the gun is produced in a vivid red color, earning the guns the "Red Glocks" nickname. The barrel bore is not drilled out, there being just a pinpoint aperture at the muzzle end, and the front of the barrel is also drilled through three times to indicate that the barrel isn't a firing version.

But red isn't the only color in the Glock training model swatch. There is also the "Blue Glock," or more

GLOCK 22P	
CALIBER:	.40
LENGTH:	8.03in (204mm)
HEIGHT:	5.43in (138mm)
WIDTH:	1.18in (30mm)
LENGTH BETWEEN SIGHTS:	6.50in (165mm)
BARREL HEIGHT:	1.26in (32mm)
BARREL LENGTH:	4.48in (114mm)
WEIGHT (UNLOADED):	22.75oz (645g)
WEIGHT (LOADED):	34.22oz (970g)
TRIGGER PULL:	~5.5lb (~2.5kg)
TRIGGER TRAVEL:	~0.49in (~12.5mm)
BARREL RIFLING:	-
RIFLING LENGTH OF TWIST:	-
MAGAZINE CAPACITY (STANDARD):	15
MAGAZINE CAPACITY (OPTIONAL):	17

specifically the G17 T. One of the key advances in tactical firearms training over the past two decades has been the emergence of effective "simunitions," non-lethal ammunition that can be used against live human beings to give realism and accuracy feedback in training scenarios. The Blue Glock is provided in two cartridges, 9mm FX and 7.8x21AC, the bullet component being either a color marker (which explodes with a definite mark on impact with the target) or a rubber component, the propellant being compressed gas. Using such ammunition, the user can engage in tactical engagements against live human opponents at up to 27 yards (25m) range, safe in the knowledge that an accurate hit will impart nothing more than a stinging pain and/or a colorful splat. (Protective clothing, particularly eye protection, is critical for anyone using simunitions, however.) In other regards, the training Glocks handle just like the real thing, although without the harsh report of a live supersonic shot.

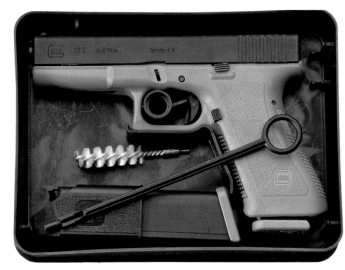

GLOCK 17 T
DATE:
1996
CALIBER:
9mm
WEIGHT (EMPTY):
18oz (510g)
LENGTH:
7.95in (202mm)
BARREL LENGTH:
4.48in (114mm)
MAGAZINE CAPACITY (STANDARD):
17
EFFECTIVE RANGE:
27yds (25m)

LEFT: The Glock 22P practice pistol was developed to eliminate dangerous scenarios during training exercises. Identical to other Glock pistols in handling, weight, size, and balance, it offers a full training experience but without the firing capability.

GLOCK 17 R

DATE:
N/A
CALIBER:
9mm
WEIGHT (EMPTY):
22.2oz (630g)
LENGTH:
8.03in (204mm)
BARREL LENGTH:
4.49in (114mm)
**MAGAZINE CAPACITY
(STANDARD):**
17

The last of the training models for the Glock is the G17 R—"Reset." This gun, which also has a red frame, is designed for use against a shooter simulator. Modern computerized simulators are ideal "shoot/don't shoot" training devices, as they project acted-out scenarios onto a large screen but enable the trainee to interact with the action via the gun. The G17 R is designed so that it can be fitted with a laser impulse generator into the barrel, which delivers a virtual shot into the screen, and accurately shows where the shot lands. The "Reset" term refers to the gun's ability to reset the trigger automatically without having to manipulate the slide; in some simulator guns, the hammer has to be reset manually before the next simulated shot can be taken. By making the hammer reset an automatic function, the G17 R enhances the realism of the training scenario, as in real combat a single shot is rare, whereas multiple shots tend to be the norm.

Loading and Firing

The Glock is not a difficult gun to handle and fire by any criteria of assessment. One of the factors that has

RIGHT: The square profile of the magazine notch here indicates that it is a drop-free magazine type.

made the gun so popular is its intuitive handling, which enables the user
to start sending rounds down range within minutes of unboxing a new gun.
Here we will just describe the basic mechanical processes of loading and
firing the gun; later in the chapter we will look in more detail at actual firing
technique and tactical handling.

The first stage in shooting a Glock is to load it. First, a magazine needs
to be charged with ammunition, the user pressing down the cartridges onto
the magazine feed plate, against the pressure of the magazine spring, so that
they are held in place by the feed lips. The base of each cartridge leads the
reloading, and the rounds are fed in from the front. Each new Glock gun
comes with a magazine loading support device, a plastic sleeve that slots over
the top of the magazine and enables the user to take some of the tension
off the magazine spring with thumb pressure when feeding in new rounds.
The loading support device is particularly recommended for use with new
magazines, which have brand new springs, full of resistance. To use the
support, it is first fitted on the top of the magazine. Then, using the thumb,
the operator presses down on the device, this forcing down the magazine
feed plate and thereby creating a gap into which the next cartridge can be
inserted easily. While pushing the round downward, the operator then slides
the loading support device upward, and the cartridge then slides to the back
of the magazine and comes to rest against the feed lips at the top.

Many shooters like to preserve magazine spring tension by avoiding filling
the magazine to capacity, stopping one or two rounds short of the maximum.
Once a magazine is filled, it can be inserted into the magazine well in the
grip, and pushed up until it fully engages with the magazine release catch.
If it isn't fully latched, the magazine indicator on the right-hand side of the
frame will protrude slightly, instead of sitting flush.

To chamber the first round, the shooter now grips the slide at the rear,
pulls it back to its further extent, then releases it. The slide now goes forward
under the full force of the return spring, strips the uppermost round from
the magazine and chambers it. Unlike many other guns, the Glock has no
external safety switch to engage at this point—it relies on its internal safeties
to make it secure. Because of this, the Glock can actually now be holstered,
ready for action with the firing pin is held under partial tension by the firing
pin spring.

Once cocked, the weapon can be fired, which requires nothing more
than putting the sights on target and pulling the trigger through its full

BELOW: **The view down
through the open slide of
a Glock 17, showing an
inspection round about to
be chambered.**

ABOVE: The Glock slide is held to the rear after the last shot in the magazine; slide release is either by depressing the release lever or recocking and releasing the slide manually.

range of movement. This action both cocks and then releases the firing pin, detonating a cartridge, the recoil force of which cycles the gun through the extraction and ejection phase, while the recoil spring then returns the gun to battery. The shooter simply keeps shooting until the magazine is empty. When it is empty, the slide will usually be held atop the rear by the slide release catch on the left side of the gun. The gun now requires a fresh magazine, and the slide released to continue firing.

There are two ways that the slide can be released from the open position. The first is to depress the slide release catch, but the one advocated by many shooters is to grip the rear of the slide, pull it a short distance to the rear and then let go. This action both disengages the slide-release catch and also gives the slide the full forward momentum of the recoil spring, ensuring efficient chambering of the cartridge.

Sights

So as we can see, there is nothing complex about shooting the Glock. We now need to consider how the Glock is sighted. Pistol sights have been through something of a revolution over the past 50 years. Many of the post-war pistols had little more than a fixed front steel blade plus a rear notch, with little to augment their user-friendliness in terms of low-light shooting or windage/elevation adjustment. All that has now changed. Today's handguns can be seen with every variety of sight options, from the familiar notch and post through to night-vision scopes and red-dot sights. Glock has kept pace with these changes—or in many cases set the pace—in everything from its standard fixed sights through to sighting accessories.

The sights that come as standard with a Glock are of the fixed variety, made of polymer. At the front of the slide is a flat-sided pyramidal affair, with a white dot in the center of the shooter's vision. The rear sight reaches across the width of the slide, and has a square-corner U-shaped notch through which the front post is aligned. The notch is outlined in white to provide quicker and more accurate sight alignment. Some users, especially competition shooters, have concerns about the long-term durability of the polymer sights, but Glock can also provide fixed steel sights as an option.

BELOW: The standard front sight post of a Glock 17 Gen3. Note the eye focus on the front, but also the correct equal light gaps either side of the post.

Although I have used the word "fixed," in reality the Glock rear sight can be adjusted side-to-side slightly for windage. To perform this a special rear-sight adjustment tool is required, which locks over the sight and uses a screw device to push the sight across in either direction. Furthermore, Glock provides both the polymer and the steel rear sights in various heights to compensate for the different ammunition characteristics in terms of trajectory and point of impact. The polymer sights come in 0.24 inches (6.1mm), 0.25 inches (6.5mm), 0.27 inches (6.9mm), and 0.29 inches (7.3mm), while the steel varieties are available in all apart from the 0.27-inch (6.9mm) version. Although specific types of sight are recommended for certain caliber guns, the shooter can fit any of the types if he wants to raise or lower his point of impact. Each increase in height typically raises the point of impact by 2 inches (50mm) at 25 yards (23m).

For those shooters who want a bit more adjustable precision to their shooting, Glock also manufacture a fully adjustable rear sight. In overall configuration this is roughly the same as the fixed sights, but the point of impact can be fine-tuned for both windage and elevation by turning screw adjusters on the side of the sight using a special adjusting tool or slender screwdriver.

ABOVE: The rear sight of the same gun. On more modern Glocks, the two white posts have been replaced by a square white frame.

As Glocks are used as frontline tactical guns by both police and military personnel, low-light shooting is a consideration for many. Although the white-edged notch and the white dot on the front post stand out reasonably well when light levels drop, if it becomes too gloomy they can become rather

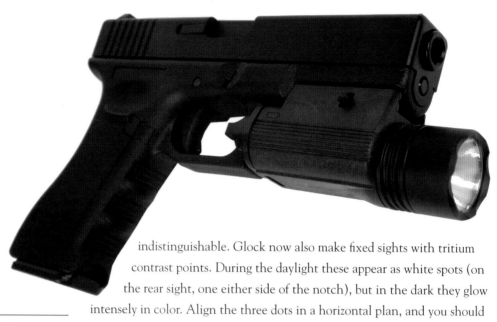

indistinguishable. Glock now also make fixed sights with tritium contrast points. During the daylight these appear as white spots (on the rear sight, one either side of the notch), but in the dark they glow intensely in color. Align the three dots in a horizontal plan, and you should be on target.

GLOCK GTL 10

TACTICAL LIGHT

HEIGHT:
2.01 inches (51mm)
LENGTH:
3.10 inches (78.5mm)
WIDTH:
1.2 inches (31mm)
**WEIGHT WITHOUT
BATTERIES:**
1.8 ounces (52g)
**WEIGHT WITH
BATTERIES:**
~3 ounces (~85g)

LIGHT:
RANGE:
328 feet (100m)
FOCUSABLE:
Yes
LIGHT:
Xenon
DIMMABLE:
No

With the introduction of the accessory rail beneath the Glock's front end in the Gen3 onward, those wanting to maximize the tactical capability of the Glock now have a few other sighting options available to them. Glock produces a range of tactical lights. The GTL 10 is the base model, formed in a rigid polymer case and holding a 6V Xenon light with 70 lumens output and an effective illumination range of 328 feet (100m). A basic tactical light is an effective aiming tool in itself in low-light, smoky, or dusty environments. The narrow beam of the torch can be directed onto the target—hence the target is lit roughly on the point of aim.

But there are more advanced models of tactical light available. Next up in the Glock range are the GTL 21 and GTL 22. Both of these accessories feature laser pointer sights set beneath the conventional white light. The lasers can be zeroed exactly to the point of impact, and the GTL 22 has the added feature of a dimmer switch to alter the intensity of the light. The top of the range models are the GTL 51 and GTL 52. Again, these modules feature the white light and laser pointer, but with the added tactical feature of an infrared laser, which is only visible through infrared night-vision goggles. Again, the difference between the models is that the GTL 52 features a dimmer switch. Note, however, that in the United States, the GTK 51 and GTL 52 are only available to law-enforcement and military users.

Basic Handling

Here is not the place to provide an in-depth guide to handgun technique. What we can do, however, is discuss some of the fundamentals of handling the Glock well, and in so doing reveal key features of the weapon that have made it the choice of more than 2.5 million users globally.

First we start with the grip angle. The Glock's grip angle is one of its defining elements. In many other pistols, particularly those based on the M1911 model, the grip is almost as a right-angle to the frame, but with the Glock the grip is noticeably raked, to an angle of 22 degrees from the vertical. The thinking behind this grip angle is that it provides an intuitive pointability to the shot, and reduces the need for the shooter to have to take considered aim to place a shot on target. In essence, the grip angle allows the shooter to punch his fist out toward the target in a natural way, and in so doing find himself roughly on target. It has been pointed out that the Glock grip basically configures the hand like a martial artist does to punch, with the two uppermost knuckles being the impact point of the blow.

The benefits of the angular grip will, of course, be undone if the user holds the Glock with a poor grip technique. As we have seen in the earlier chapters, the Glocks come in all manner of sizes, from big 10mm brutes

FACING PAGE: Tactical lights offer both target illumination and enhanced target acquisition, although they are no substitute for good general gun handling.

BELOW: A poor grip—note how the top of the hand sits well below the tang, a hold that will increase muzzle flip and the chance of gun malfunction.

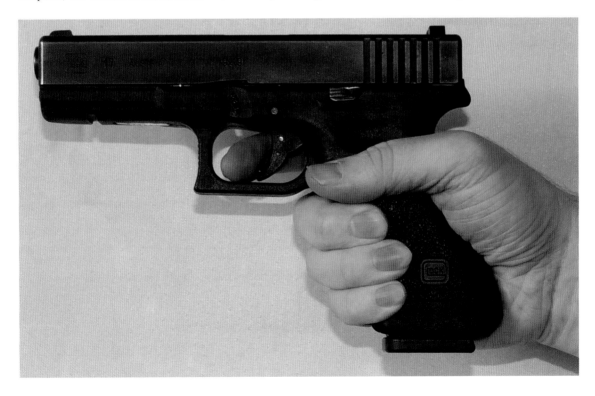

RIGHT: An improved grip—the gun hand is pushed right up to the tang, and the thumb runs along the frame just beneath the slide.

down to pocketable .380 Autos. Yet the basic grip principles remain the same. For real accuracy from a handgun, the two-handed grip is by far the best. Before describing how this is best put together, it needs to be acknowledged that the Glock can be fired successfully one-handed. All Glocks have a low-bore axis, which essentially means that if you drew a line through the center of the bore and continued out through the back of the slide, that line would sit close to the top of your hand. This in turn means that the force of recoil in the gun is closer to the hand, and therefore the recoil is easier to absorb and control. Guns with a higher bore axis induce more "flip" during recoil, requiring a stronger grip resistance and a longer return to the point of aim.

Because the Glock has a relatively controllable recoil, even in the big calibers, one-handed shooting is viable. It is facilitated even more by the fact that the gun doesn't have an external safety, so one hand alone can make the shot, and the same hand can also operate the magazine release when necessary.

Yet for real accuracy, the two-handed grip is the key. First, wrap your gun hand (as opposed to your supporting hand) around the grip, pushing the soft part of the hand between the thumb and the fingers high up against the gun's tang, to get as close to the bore axis as possible. The grip is squeezed

firmly from front to back, although not so tightly that it introduces a tension tremble in the hand or arm. The thumb of the grip hand is kept high and running forward along the side of the frame just below the slide, pointing in the direction of the target. You should notice a gap between the grip-hand fingers and thumb on the grip, and into this space slot the thumb of your supporting hand, like a jigsaw piece dropping into place. The supporting hand fingers wrap around the grip-hand fingers, but squeeze inward onto the sides of the grip. What this means is that the Glock grip is now supported under tension from 360 degrees, making the whole structure extremely stable. The supporting hand thumb lies underneath and alongside the other thumb in a spoon-like pairing, while the padded area beneath the thumb presses in against the grip plate.

Now the grip is complete. Although this grip might feel odd for those used to other approaches, it is the one advocated by most tactical instructors and combat shooters. It maximizes the area of flesh pressed against the gun, which in turn means that the gun is held in a very stable relation to the body.

One of the strengths of the Glock for tactical shooting, in which shots must be put on target in rapid succession to ensure a take-down, is the trigger pull. When you put your finger on a Glock trigger and start to pull it back, there is about 0.4 inches (10mm) of mechanical slack, during which there is almost no resistance to the trigger pull. At this point the trigger will then meet definite resistance, as the trigger bar comes into contact with the angled ramp of the connector, and just another 0.13 inches (3mm) of pull will produce a shot. It is a crisp, clean, and controllable action. What is more significant, however, is that letting the trigger out again by just about 0.13 inches (3mm) will reset the trigger for the next shot, meaning that multiple shots can be delivered extremely quickly with good trigger control.

Gaining such trigger control takes practice in "constant contact" mode—meaning that the trigger finger remains in contact with the trigger through both the draw and the release phase, rather than coming off the trigger to allow it to reset. As Glock demonstration shooters show, the gun can literally be emptied as fast as you can pull the trigger. Considering that the Glock has such high-capacity magazines, this means that the shooter can put very substantial amounts of fire onto a given target very quickly.

Sighting and Stance

Stance and sighting are usually discussed as separate issues, but in reality the two are intrinsically linked. But I need to define what I mean by "stance," and how it relates to the Glock. There is much debate among firearms trainers about the optimal position from which to shoot a handgun. Some advocate the Weaver stance, while other vigorously advocate an isosceles position, or a personal combination of the two. In reality, apart from in the case of meticulous stationary target shooting, a stance is a dynamic affair, the shooter having to adjust his or her body and aiming position constantly depending on the needs of the shot. What is critical, therefore, is that the basic grip is solid and well-formed and that the shooter has a high degree of trigger control. With both of these fundamentals in place, the shooter will be able to focus attention on sighting the pistol accurately and fluidly.

When sighting the Glock using the standard iron sights, the normal principles of handgun marksmanship apply. The front post should sit squarely in the rear sight notch, the top of the post aligned with the top of the notch and with an equal amount of light seen either side of the post, if at all. The point of aim is aligned with both of these elements. If the rear sight has white dots on each pillar, then the accurate sight picture should have three dots aligned from side to side in equal measure. Here lies a problem. The human eye can essentially only focus on one point at

a time. When sighting, therefore, the untrained eye is constantly flicking back and forward between rear sight-front sight-target, a situation that produces visual confusion and a lack of concentration on the actual point of aim. With the Glock, therefore, it is best to concentrate most of all on the front sight, ensuring that this point sits directly on where you want the bullet to go. If your grip has been trained properly, the gun should be fairly well aligned anyway, using the "pointability" at which the Glock excels.

ABOVE: Tori Nonaka of Team Glock demonstrates a perfectly balanced stance; note the slight lean forward to counteract recoil.

ABOVE: Here a G18 lets fly with a full-auto burst; the shooter adopts the "Weaver" stance, with a locked gun arm and a bent supporting arm.

Of course, the situation becomes more complicated once the light levels drop. Training in low-light shooting is critical for law-enforcement officers, military personnel, and all those who are serious about self-defense, as some 70 percent of all lethal encounters happen at night. Two things can happen to the shooter in low-light conditions. First, the eye's peripheral vision works better than central vision under conditions of darkness, and the tactical result of this physiological effect is that shooters often end up aiming low on their target. Second, the waters are muddied by the fact that the front post of the gun can all too easily blend into the dark silhouettes and shadowy forms of the poorly lit target, making the shooter lose awareness of both the gun alignment and the target.

The Glock has several useful design features that help tactical shooters cope with low-light shooting. We again return to the gun's pointability. In the way that the gun naturally aligns itself with the grip arm, the shooter will more instinctively know when the gun is on target, even without direct feedback from the sights. Trusting the human body's natural capacity to point at things accurately should be part of training with the Glock, as the gun is well suited to this "instinctive shooting" technique. If the Glock sights have luminous inserts, then the shooter will have a three-dot system for providing aim information. It has been argued that this system could present a problem in which, by pointing the muzzle too far to the left or right, the shooter could see three targeting dots perfectly aligned without realizing that the dot to the extreme left or right is actually the front post. Theoretically, this seems possible, but this error only seems likely in those with extremely little experience of using the handgun and of its sight picture. If the gun were so misaligned, the shooter should notice a difference in the spacing intervals between the dots. Furthermore, even if the shooter was in virtual pitch darkness, he would probably sense the angling of the wrist away from the target, working against the intended direction of the gun.

ABOVE: An Iraqi policeman practices firing his Glock pistol from a kneeling position. The body weight should be a little more forward, into the recoil.

Laser Sights

We have already discussed the option of fitting a laser pointer device to the handgun. With one of these in place, low-light shooting presents far less of the problem. Indeed, such is the brightness of a laser pointer system that they can also be used in full daylight, and unless the target is washed in direct and very bright sunlight, the laser signature will still be seen.

GLOCK 38
WITH QD LASER
DATE:
Late 1990s
CALIBER:
.45 GAP
WEIGHT (EMPTY WITH LASER):
30.43oz (863g)
LENGTH:
7.36in (187mm)
BARREL LENGTH:
4.01in (102mm)
MAGAZINE CAPACITY (STANDARD):
8
EFFECTIVE RANGE:
40yds (37m)

A shooter needs to spend some time practicing with a laser targeting system if it is to make a valuable contribution to the Glock. First, it needs to be accurately zeroed. Here you have two options. One option is to zero the laser to the actual bullet impact point at a specified distance, say 25 yards (23m), in much the same way as the telescopic sight on a rifle is zeroed. This approach has its problems. A rifle scope will usually have graduated reticules, so that the shooter can make a conscious adjustment of the point of impact for different ranges. With a pistol this isn't possible, so at ranges above and beyond the zero the laser will not accurately show the impact point. Some shooters might not feel that this is a problem, but another (possibly better?) option is to have the laser parallel to the bore axis. This means that the laser beam will be about 1 inch (2.5cm) under the point of impact, but that is a predictable quantity to deal with. Furthermore, as the bullet drops over range it will actually fall toward the laser point. So, put the laser roughly center on the target's torso, and you will be guaranteed a significant hit.

Laser sights can be regarded as devices that render good gun control and proper aiming technique redundant—simply put the dot on the target and pull the trigger. Such is not the case. Laser points flicker around quickly on the target, especially if that target is moving, and the laser dot can become a distraction that retards the speed of shot if it is given too much focus. Far better to acquire the target with a confident aiming of the gun itself, and let the laser pointer give you additional precision in the shot. This being said, laser pointers and narrow-beam tactical lights do offer genuine advantages. For example, they allow the shooter to keep the primary focus on the target activity and movement, without pulling the eyes back to look at the iron sights. They also permit aimed firing from all sorts of strange angles and positions—such as with the hand cocked around a car door—while not necessarily having to place the face directly behind the gun. Those who might have to use the Glock with such flexible positioning, however, are well advised to practice shooting from multiple different positions, safely and with the gun under full control.

ABOVE: The Glock GTL 10, a tactical light made from the same tough polymer as the Glock itself.

Tactical Lights

The Glock tactical lights are very well designed to have a minimal impact on the balance and control of the weapon. By having the batteries vertically stacked inside, instead of side-by-side, the lights are very slender and don't encroach much beyond the width of the slide. They also offer excellent controls for adapting the functions to exactly what is required. The controls on the GTL 22, for example, allow the user to select off, light only, light and laser, and laser only positions, and the beam of the torch can be narrowed or opened by turning the movable ring around the lens. The lights are also extremely easy to fit, simply sliding onto the front rail and clicking solidly into place via a spring-loaded bar on the top of the light engaging with a corresponding groove running underneath the rail mount, the body of the light tucking up securely around the front of the trigger guard.

Removing is equally easy—just press down the release catches on each side of the light, which drops the locking bar and allows the light to slide off.

One point to note about fitting the tactical lights is that while the same light can be fitted to multiple Gen3 and Gen4 models, installing one on the more compact models might mean that the front of the light projects ahead of the muzzle. While there is no actual danger to the light unit, it does expose it to more flash and smoke, hence the light will become dirty more quickly than if it is installed on a full-size Glock such as the G17, where the light and laser lens are protected beneath the frame. The light units with adjustable beam strength are particularly good—the dimmer capability has a genuine tactical use. By putting the beam on a low-lighting level, the user both preserves much of his own night-vision capability, plus doesn't advertise his position as strongly to a potential adversary. When the moment requires full brightness, a simple tap on the rear switch with the trigger finger can give you intense illumination.

GLOCK PENETRATION	
.40 CALIBER, 4IN (102MM) BARREL:	• Winchester 0.42oz (12g, 180-grain) JHP, velocity 990ft/sec (302m/sec), energy 390 ft/lb (529 J), penetration 12.20in (310mm), expansion 0.65in (16.51mm)
	• Federal 0.42oz (12g, 180-grain) Hydra-Shok, velocity 985ft/sec (300m/sec), energy 384ft/lb (521 J), penetration 14in (355.6mm), expansion 0.69in (17.5mm)
	• Winchester 0.35oz (10g, 155-grain) SilverTip HP, velocity 1,205ft/sec (367m/sec), energy 500ft/lb (678 J), penetration 12.7in (322.5mm), expansion 0.6in (15.24mm)
0.39IN (10MM), 5IN (127MM) BARREL:	• (FBI) Federal 0.42oz (12g, 180-grain) JHP, velocity 931ft/sec (284m/sec), energy 346ft/lb (469 J), penetration 17.24in (437.9mm), expansion 0.547in (11.6mm)
	• Winchester 0.42oz (12g, 180-grain) JHP, velocity 955ft/sec (291m/sec), energy 364ft/lb (494 J), penetration 16.61in (421.9mm), expansion 0.526in (13.4mm)
	• Norma 0.39oz (11g, 170-grain) JHP, velocity 1,358ft/sec (414m/sec), energy 696ft/lb (944 J), penetration 18.44in (468.4mm), expansion 0.562in (14.2mm)
.45 ACP, (5IN) BARREL:	• Remington 0.42oz (12g, 185-grain) JHP, velocity 903ft/sec (275m/sec), energy 334ft/lb (453 J), penetration 22.21in (564.1mm), expansion 0.54in (13.7mm)
	• Federal 0.42oz (12g, 185-grain) JHP, velocity 953ft/sec (290m/sec), energy 373 ft/lb (506 J), penetration 13.62in (345.9mm), expansion 0.623in (15.8mm)
	• Winchester 0.42oz (12g, 185-grain) Silvertip JHP, velocity 951ft/sec (290m/sec), energy 371ft/lb (503 J), penetration 13.58in (344.9mm), expansion 0.619in (15.7mm)
	• Federal 0.53oz (15g, 230-grain) Hydra-Shok, velocity 802ft/sec (244m/sec), energy 328ft/lb (445 J), penetration 18.28in (464.3mm), expansion 0.621in (15.7mm)

Reloading

On professional tactical handgun training, as much time is often spent instructing in fast reloading as it is on actual shooting technique. The reason for this is transparent. When you are reloading, you are not shooting, hence this could be the moment when an attacker who still has rounds in his gun can take the advantage. Therefore the reloading action on the Glock needs to be practiced until it is rapid and fluid, and takes only a second or so to get back into action. We have already noted that Glock magazines come in two varieties—those that drop free of the gun as soon as the mag release is pressed, and those that stay in the gun and need to be drawn free with the non-shooting hand. Naturally these two configurations demand a different approach to the reloading process. (Note that in this instance we are purely focusing on tactical reloading techniques, where speed is of the essence and the possibility of damaging the empty magazine is not necessarily a consideration.)

The signal that the gun needs reloading is usually when the slide locks back after the last round has been fired. To reload the gun, first bring the gun back into a position just in front of the chest (an area that US police trainers sometimes refer to as the "working space"). Don't try to reload the gun at arm's length, because this is physically more awkward. Nor should you allow the gun to drop lower than your chest. If you do so, your eyes are therefore pointing down when they should remain up and studying how the tactical situation is developing. Also, by training yourself to reload without having to look at the gun, you can keep your eyes on the target and therefore have immediate target acquisition after the reload.

LEFT: Magazines for the Glock either drop free when the mag release is pressed or, like here, need to be drawn physically out from the gun.

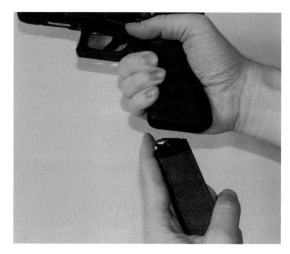

ABOVE AND RIGHT: The Glock mag release sits just at the top of the grip. Touching the uppermost round with the tip of the index finger makes it easier to find the mag well.

BELOW: Ensure you seat the magazine firmly, so that you hear the mag catch click to engage.

To exchange a non-drop magazine, there are two basic methods:

1. Press the magazine release button with the thumb (if you are right-handed) or with the forefinger (left-handed).

2. Reach up with the non-gun hand and grasp the magazine baseplate. Pull the magazine from the grip and either let it fall or, in non life-threatening situations, retain.

3. Grasp a fresh magazine from your magazine pouch. Whenever you hold a fresh magazine for the reload, extend your index finger up the front of the magazine, so that the tip of the finger is touching the bullet of 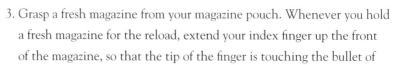 the uppermost round of ammunition. By doing this you not only ensure that you have the magazine facing in the right direction, but the finger tip also provides a guide for finding the magazine well accurately. In addition, when shooting under low-light conditions, the finger-tip check ensures that you have actually picked up a fully loaded magazine, and not an empty that you put back in your magazine pouch earlier.

4. Feed the magazine into the bottom of the magazine well and drive it home until it clicks into place.

5. Now either press the slide release to send the slide forward to chamber a round, or wrap the non-gun hand over the top of the slide, palm down, and ratchet and release the slide.

Even though this process has five distinctive stages, with practice it can be performed in little more than two seconds, so the tactical downtime is minimal. If the magazine is of the drop type, the process is even quicker. In essence, you repeat the process above but, because you don't have to pull the empty magazine out, you can reach for an fresh magazine at the same time as you press the magazine release, letting the empty mag simply drop out onto the floor.

In some circumstances, you might want to retain the empty magazine, or a partially empty magazine. There are several methods of doing this, some of which require a certain amount of manual dexterity hence won't be described in laborious detail here. There are, however, two rough options. First, you simply extract the empty magazine, put it away, then load a new mag. Second—as a quicker method with non-drop magazines—you press the mag release while retrieving a new mag and then do a quick switch between the mags using either the gun hand and the free hand working together or, if you are nimble enough, extracting and holding the spent mag then feeding in the new mag from the same hand. All these techniques can be found in the plentiful Glock videos online, or by observing competition shooters at work, who tend to be masters of fast reloading techniques.

Malfunctions

The Glock wouldn't have gained the reputation it has if it had proved itself unreliable in service. Both in trials and in operations the Glock has, with some hiccups and controversies, largely asserted itself as a dependable sidearm. Nevertheless, stoppages occur in all firearms, and the Glock is no exception in this regard. In this chapter, we will therefore look in some detail at the things that stop a Glock functioning during the stages of its operating cycle.

First, however, we can make some generic advice about handling a sudden Glock stoppage, applicable to most semi-auto handguns and officially advocated by Glock. Picture the scene. You are stood at the stand on the range, working smoothly through a magazine's worth of Glock cartridges, when the gun just gives an ominous click rather than a satisfying bang. The first response is to take your finger off the trigger and exercise muzzle control—keep the muzzle pointing in a safe direction, as the problem might be a "hangfire." Here the primer has been struck but instead of a instant detonation, the main propellant is smoldering until it reaches detonation pressure. Such an occurrence can result in the gun suddenly firing several seconds after pulling the trigger, so keep your grip firm while maintaining a down-range muzzle angle. If, after about five seconds, nothing has happened, you should proceed to clear the gun.

The simplest and the quickest method of gun clearance is what is catchily called the "tap, rack, and bang" technique. First, give the magazine baseplate a firm push with the base of the hand, to ensure that the magazine is properly seated and isn't causing feed issues. Second, grab the slide with an overhand grip (meaning the hand isn't behind the slide, in case there is a sudden discharge), and pull it back to its further extent and release. As you do this, you might eject a faulty or misfed round, and all being well you will chamber the next round in the magazine and then be able to resume your shooting.

If this is not successful, then you might have to do more detailed clearance procedures. First, release the magazine from the gun by pressing the mag release button. With the magazine out of the gun, then pull the slide backward to clear a chambered or misfed cartridge, and lock the slide at the rear. Now visually inspect the gun for problems, and if nothing obvious is spotted then proceed to reload the gun, release the slide, and resume shooting. If there are still problems, then either you have a defective batch of ammunition or there is some internal problem that requires full-blown maintenance.

BELOW: In the case of a misfeed, follow the "tap, rack, bang" procedure to clear and keep shooting.

Feed Problems

Feed problems refer to any issue affecting the smooth transition of a cartridge from the top of the magazine to the chamber, whereupon the gun should be locked up and ready to fire. An easily solved issue is that the magazine is not seated properly. This is actually a common issue, given that the Glock magazines can fit tightly in the gun's grip. When loading the gun, listen out for an audible click as the magazine fully engages with the release catch, then give the magazine a pull on the baseplate to ensure that the mag is locked in soldier. You can also observe that the plastic part of the release catch on the right-hand side of the grip is flush with the frame; if it isn't, this means that the magazine has not connected properly.

LEFT: The barrel block should sit flush with the slide aperture when the gun has properly chambered a round.

Another cause of a failure to feed is if the magazine has been damaged in some way. The types of damage are varied—deformed feed lips, bulges in the magazine tube, and weakened magazine springs. The last two of these problems can both be the result of overloading the magazine, squeezing in that extra round but overloading both the spring and the tube at the same time. If you suspect the magazine is the problem, simply try another magazine and see if the problem rectifies itself.

Feed problems are not just centered on the magazine. Sometimes a cartridge is stripped or partially stripped from the magazine and doesn't chamber properly. This problem can be visually obvious—the slide will either be jammed back, clearly showing the stuck cartridge through the ejection port, or the barrel block won't be sitting flush with the top of the slide. The cause of this sort of misfeed is likely to be either faulty ammunition or dirt in the gun mechanism, such as on the slide rails or the feed ramp. The basic gun-clearance procedures outlined above are the quickest ways to get through such a jam and keep shooting, but if the problem persist it is likely that the gun needs to be stripped and cleaned, or

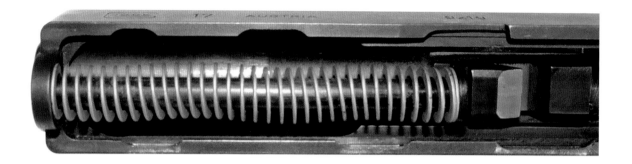

ABOVE: A view of the Glock recoil spring sitting within the slide housing. The cam surfaces of the barrel are seen to the right.

the brand/batch of ammunition needs changing. What is not recommended is trying to force the slide forward to chamber the round; this impatient measure is likely to increase the problematic nature of the stoppage, and mean that more substantial maintenance is required to fix it.

There are some other mechanical causes of misfeed, such as weakened recoil springs. But sometimes a misfire can result in the gun failing to perform its recoil and reloading cycle properly. In the case of a squib cartridge—one with insufficient powder in it—the bullet might be forced out of the case but then become wedged in the barrel, causing in turn the gun to fail to go through its recoil cycle properly, or leaving a dangerous obstruction in the bore. While shooting the Glock, if you experience any unusual reports on firing, cease shooting immediately and make a thorough visual and physical inspection of the gun.

Firing Problems

Squib cartridges and hangfires, already discussed in this chapter, are two issues that can also cause firing problems in a Glock. Thankfully, these issues are relatively rare if high-quality ammunition is purchased from a reputable manufacturer. However, the easy accessibility of cheap ammunition from places such as China, Eastern Europe, or Pakistan means that such malfunctions are still experienced. So the moral of the story is to buy the best ammunition that you can afford. High-quality ammunition also tends to provide the power required to drive a gun consistently through its operating cycle.

Another reason a Glock might not fire is that there is a mechanical malfunction, specifically with the firing-pin mechanism being broken or damaged. This problem, it has to be said, is extremely rare, and is often the result of the pin hitting a foreign body or a problematic type of ammunition. For example, in May 2013 some reports emerged in the United States

that the Palm Beach County Sheriff's Department was experiencing Glock misfires. On inspection, it was discovered that the firing pins of the malfunctioning guns were cracked or chipped. However, there was a curious pattern behind the problems—they only occurred during indoor training sessions. As it turned out, during the training sessions the police unit was using non-toxic ammunition, which had harder primers than standard ammunition, and this was causing damage to the firing pins. A quick adjustment by Glock and the problem was resolved.

In some guns, replacing a firing pin is the type of job suited to an experienced gunsmith. In the Glock, however, it is relatively straightforward to disassemble the firing-pin assembly and replace the damaged part, although the process does take some manual dexterity and strong fingers. (See the Glock manual for a full description of this process.) As noted, however, problems with the firing pin in Glocks are very rare, and you are likely to use a Glock for its entire working life on the original firing pin.

ABOVE: A stiff grip on the Glock is essential if you are to avoid some of the feed problems associated with "limp-wristing."

FACING PAGE, TOP: As the Glock is cocked, the barrel chamber block drops down out of alignment with the slide ejection port.

Extraction and Ejection Problems

Problems with extraction and ejection can cause some of the more stubborn variety of jams and malfunctions in a Glock. On the extraction side of the equation, a failure to extract essentially means that the extractor has not caught the case of the spent cartridge efficiently, and leaves it in the chamber. This causes a double malady if another cartridge is then stripped from the magazine and the gun attempts to chamber it. The tip of the new cartridge becomes jammed against the base of the chambered case, with the combined pressure from both the magazine spring and recoil spring holding the whole problem locked firmly into place.

Although the double-feed can, for those unfamiliar with it, appear to defy all manner of efforts to clear it, in reality the process can be quite straightforward. In fact, applying the "tap, rack, and bang" process outlined above can shake out some double feeds. If the problem proves to be stubborn, press the magazine release catch and draw out the magazine, then rack the slide repeatedly until the problem clears. Then reload and shoot away. Note that in most other semi-auto handguns, clearing a double-feed first requires the slide to be locked back before the magazine can drop out.

While the double-feed is alarming enough, particularly in a tactical emergency, a failure to eject a cartridge properly can also be a cause for anxiety, albeit momentary. A failure to eject means that the spent case is extracted properly from the chamber, but it is not thrown clear of the gun. The outcome of this problem is often that the slide attempts to return to battery, but it catches the spent case and jams it in the ejection port, a problem typically known as a "stovepipe," from the appearance of the empty case pointing upright.

The primary cause of a stovepipe is often nothing to do with the ejector itself. Instead, a slide returning forward early is often the root problem, the causes of which are multiple. For example, if the Glock is firing underpowered ammunition, the slide might not be driven fully backward before it begins its return journey, catching the spent casing before it makes it out of the gun. Ironically, but more rarely, the problem can also result from overpowerful ammunition driving the slide back so hard it bounces forward from the stops with extra speed. A dirty gun might also be vulnerable to failures to eject, but the issue might even lie with the shooter rather than the gun. All semi-automatic handguns require a certain amount of grip resistance if they are to function properly. If the grip on the gun is too weak, or if it is

FACING PAGE, BOTTOM: If the barrel block is out of alignment when you have loaded the gun, it likely means the cartridge isn't properly seated.

too far below the tang, essentially the hand becomes a hinge around which the whole gun pivots during the recoil phase. What now happens is that the slide and the frame move back almost together, rather than the slide driving back on its own, resulting in the slide not opening far enough to eject the spent case; the case becomes trapped in the partial slide return.

The remedy for this problem, pointedly referred to as "limp-wristing," has nothing to do with the gun and everything to do with grip. Make sure that you have the gun in a firm, high grip, with the grip hand right up against the upper curve of the gun's tang. Brace the wrist firmly, although do not press down in anticipation of the recoil, as this is a common cause for sending rounds low. Another reason for grip-related slide/ejection malfunctions might be from having one or both of the thumbs resting against the slide, and interfering with its free movement. Check the side of the gun before firing, to ensure that the thumbs are clear of slide movement. (Following the principles of Glock grip outlined above will go a long way to avoiding limp-wristing or thumb-to-slide malfunctions.)

Clearing the stovepipe is simply a matter of following the "tap, rack, and bang" process outlined above. Note that the "rack" part of the equation is essential. Even though you can pull back the slide a little to clear the stovepipe, this does not reload a fresh cartridge, so make sure you pull the slide back to its fullest extent before releasing.

Maintenance

The Glock's ability to absorb all manner of punishment, from sub-zero temperatures to being dragged behind cars, is well known. But we must not take the point too far. All guns, even absolute workhorses such as the AK-47, will eventually malfunction if they are not given a basic level of maintenance. Fortunately, Glock has designed a series of guns that are simplicity itself to strip, clean, and reassemble.

So when should you strip and clean your Glock? The official Glock advice on this matter is clear, and is expanded upon here. Strip, clean, and lubricate your gun:

1. When it is brand new, and before you take the gun to the range to fire.

2. At least once a month. Even if the gun isn't used during that period, it can be judicious to take the gun out of storage and strip it down, as some

FACING PAGE, TOP: Remove the slide by drawing it back a few millimeters (using the grip shown), then pressing down the slide, release on both sides.

FACING PAGE, BOTTOM: If the slide release has been properly engaged, the slide can be pushed off the front of the frame.

ABOVE: **A phosphor bronze brush is ideal for cleaning stubborn fouling from the the bore of a Glock.**

lubricants dry out over time. While in storage, ensure that the gun is not subject to damp or excessive cold or heat. The Glock is a tough gun, but there is no sense in unduly testing that toughness.

3. After each firing. Although modern propellants are far less "sooty" than the products of half a century ago, they still leave corrosive deposits in the barrel and the action, which will build up over time if left unchecked. An uncleaned gun, even if just left for a few days, is also more vulnerable to pitting and rust than one that is cleaned out just after the shoot.

4. Finally, clean the gun whenever it gets dirty. This doesn't just mean when the gun has been fired, but also when it has been exposed to environmental effects such as dust, dirt, rain, sea spray, lint, etc. Always ensure that your gun is free of foreign bodies.

   When performing a clean, don't be tempted to take the lazy-man's approach and simply drive a cleaning brush down the barrel from the muzzle end, with the gun assembled. Not only does this not address dirt and debris in the nooks and crannies of the action, but it can also push dirt and excess oil from the barrel into the slide and trigger workings, actually making the gun worse off than if you'd left it alone. So, you should become conversant with basic field stripping of your Glock handgun to perform proper cleaning.

Disassembly, Cleaning, and Lubrication

The Glock breaks down into five major component sections for a basic field strip:

- slide
- barrel
- recoil spring assembly
- receiver
- magazine

   The first stage of disassembling the gun into these parts is to remove the magazine and draw the slide back into its locked position, making a visual and physical inspection of the chamber to ensure that no cartridge is in place. Now, keep the muzzle of the gun pointing in a safe direction, release the slide forward, and pull the trigger to its rearmost position.

   The next stage is to remove the gun's slide. To do this you have to draw back the slide carefully for a distance of about 0.1 inches (3mm). The best

BELOW: A Glock 17 slide and recoil spring. Glock components require minimal oiling to function properly.

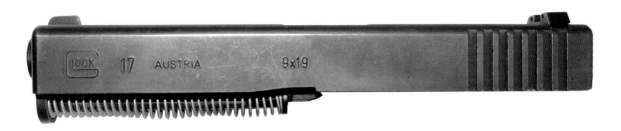

ABOVE: The Glock 17 barrel and recoil spring. The full-size Glocks have single recoil springs, while the compact models utilize dual springs.

way to do this is, with your cocking hand, wrap your thumb around the recurve part of the backstrap, to provide leverage, and draw the slide back with four fingers wrapped over the top. When you have done this, pull down the slide lock on the side of the frame using your thumb and forefinger; this action now allows you to push the slide forward and separate it from the receiver. If you find that the slide doesn't want to detach, it is probably because you have drawn the slide back too far.

You can now remove the barrel and recoil spring assembly as follows. First, push the recoil-spring assembly forward with the thumb, applying pressure on the large end of the recoil-spring tube, and raise it up and out of the slide. Be careful here—remember that the recoil spring is under tension. Therefore keep it pointing away from your face and, to be extra safe, wear eye protection. Once the recoil spring assembly has been removed, you can now take a grip on the barrel locking piece, push it slightly forward, then lift it and pull it backward out of the slide.

RIGHT: The underside of the Glock barrel, showing the large front lug that engages with the locking block.

Many people will not go the extra mile and disassemble the magazine, but this should be done periodically as well. Magazines suffer from dirt ingress just like any other part of the gun, and leaving the dirt to accumulate will eventually result in a misfeed. Like taking out the spring assembly, however, magazine disassembly needs to be approached with some caution, as the parts are under heavy spring tension and can fly out if not controlled. The process for dismantling the magazine varies slightly according the magazine type, so here it is best to consult the official Glock manuals. Once you have broken the magazine down into its parts, however, you should clean out all dirt with a dry brush, and wipe down the parts with a soft, clean cloth. Do not use lubricants in the magazine, as this can affect the ammunition.

You have now broken the gun down into its main component sections, making it accessible for cleaning. Spray a reputable bore-cleaning solvent down the barrel, allow it to soak in for a few minutes, then clean the bore through from the chamber end using a bore brush for the appropriate caliber. Then push clean patches through the bore until it is dry and spotless. On the outside of the barrel, clean away any dirt or debris from the locking surfaces using a brush or cloth.

Once the barrel is clean, you can then work systematically around the slide and frame with a toothbrush-type cleaning tool (which can in fact be a soft toothbrush) or a soft cloth dampened with solvent, cleaning around all the moving parts and surfaces of the gun. Adjust the angle of the parts of the gun as you clean, so that any dirt you dislodge doesn't just fall back into the mechanisms. After cleaning, wipe the parts down with a dry cloth to remove any residual solvent. However, in their official manuals Glock reminds its customers not to remove the copper-colored lubricant on the slide of brand-new Glocks, as this is a long-term factory-applied lubricant.

When lubricating a Glock, the key point is to apply the lubricant sparingly. Excess oil does more harm than good, attracting dirt and dust and congealing into an abrasive grinding mixture that can actually wear away at parts and hinder their smooth operation. Using a patch dampened (not soaked) with gun oil, wipe over the outside of the barrel, including the barrel hood and lugs, and also along the inside of the slide where the barrel block rubs against slide surface. Apply a single drop of oil along the length of each of the four slide rails, and also place a single drop of oil where the rear end of the trigger bar touches the connector at the right rear corner of the frame.

CHECKING SAFETY DEVICES—OFFICIAL GLOCK ADVICE

The following safety checks are to be carried out at regular intervals, e.g., before each use or when cleaning the weapon after use:

a) Function testing the trigger safety:
- Remove the magazine from your pistol and reassure that there is no cartridge in the barrel.
  Then the trigger may be pulled back.
- Bring back the trigger in its most forward position by cycling the slide. The trigger safety (lever integrated in trigger) should then be properly engaged.
- When lateral pressure is applied on the trigger the safety should keep engaged, blocking the trigger movement.
- Failure of the trigger safety to properly engage or block indicates that it is defective.

Do not reload or use your weapon again and contact GLOCK Ges.m.b.H. or an authorized GLOCK armorer immediately.

b) Function testing the firing pin safety:
- Dismantle the weapon into its main components as described previously and remove the recoil spring/recoil spring tube and barrel from the slide.
- Hold the slide in a muzzle down position and depress the firing pin safety. The tip of the firing pin should move forward and be visible protruding from the firing pin hole.
- Keep the firing pin safety depressed and shake the slide. The firing pin should be distinctly heard moving freely.
- Draw back manually the firing pin about 0.2 inches (5mm).
- Hold the slide in a horizontal position and push forward the firing pin toward the muzzle, firing pin safety being engaged.

The firing pin should not protrude from the firing pin hole. If it does, the firing pin and the firing pin safety should be replaced.

Accessories

One important point to note throughout this book is that I only describe official Glock products. This is purely for reasons of convenience—if I expanded the content to include all the non-Glock accessories that can be fitted to Glock handguns, this book would be much, much larger. However, it is worth noting that third-party manufacturers provide numerous different products that can enhance, accessorize, and maintain your Glock. These include holsters, sights (optical and iron), laser pointers, slide locks, caliber conversion kits (including .50 and .22 calibers), special magazines, compensated and extended barrels and custom magwells, and various slides and frames. If you are close to someone who is an enthusiastic Glock owner, you will rarely be short of ideas for special-day presents.

Here, however, we will look briefly at some of the official Glock accessories that can enhance your use of the gun. A few we have touched upon already—tactical lights/lasers and speed loaders specifically. For tactical handling of the guns, Glock also makes holsters. Its Sport Combat model holster is designed for mounting a Glock handgun beneath a coat or jacket for concealed carry. It can be fitted with a variety of strap widths, and it can also be worn on either side of the body for ambidextrous use. The gun is kept in place by a retention device that grips onto the trigger guard.

ABOVE: The Glock speed-loading device slots over the magazine and allows the user to take off the spring pressure by using the thumb.

The other holster type offered by Glock is the Duty Holster for wearing on the thigh. It is available in both left- and right-hand versions, with a thumb break retention strap to keep the gun securely in place. It is only designed for three specific gun types, however: the G17, G22, and G31. At the time of writing, the Glock website specifically states that the holster is not available for 10mm and .45 handguns.

One other Glock device the shooter will find useful is the Magazine Pouch, which holds a single high-capacity magazine ready for use. Like the holsters, it is made from Glock's signature polymer, making it practically indestructible.

Glock handguns are some of the most functionally effective weapons in history. What makes them the gun of choice for millions of shooters is their combination of reliability, ease of handling, their smooth contours, and their undoubted ability to put effective rounds on target. Having looked at the Glock in terms of function, it's now time to look at what the gun means to its end users, those who trust their lives to a block of metal and polymer.

Law Enforcement Use

Die Hard 2 is a justifiably popular film, full of the character and action on which the series hangs. From the perspective of the firearms historian, however, it offers a two-hour insight into the gun culture of the 1990s. Made in 1990, the movie features a high percentage of Glocks, wielded principally by the villains of the film. At one point, John McClane (played inimitably by Bruce Willis) is arguing with cop Carmine Lorenzo about the professionalism and purpose of the criminals he has just engaged. He states, during the argument: "That punk pulled a Glock 7 on me. You know what that is? It's a porcelain gun made in Germany. Doesn't show up on your airport X-ray machines here, and it cost more than you make in a month."

FACING PAGE: Police Cadet Dalia Hassan, 20, aims her 9mm G17 handgun during a shooting drill at the Baghdad Police Academy at the end of a four-week training programme.

Earlier, where we discussed the famous X-ray incident, and also noting the factual errors ("Glock 7," "porcelain gun"), there is still something fascinating about this passage. For here we see a handgun given virtual celebrity status in a movie. Not a machine gun, tank, warship, aircraft, or other great weapon system, but a humble handgun. Such was the media interest in the Glock in the late 1980s and early 1990s. Also note that the gun is placed in the hands of criminals, not the police. Here we get a sense of the double reputation that the Glock has forged. It has been represented as the both the cop's best friend and the cop's worst enemy. In this chapter, however, we focus mainly on the former, on the Glock as one of the best combat handguns issued to police since the end of World War II. The story has drama, controversy, tragedy, and misrepresentation throughout, but the outcome is undeniable. The Glock has become the world's most popular

FACING PAGE: **A Finnish competitor shoots a G19 handgun at the World Police and Fire Games.**

handgun for law-enforcement use. In the United States alone—the biggest of all the law-enforcement firearms markets—Glocks constitute about 70 percent of the handguns issued. This fact is all the more remarkable considering that Gaston Glock himself had never made a handgun before the Glock 17.

The Police Requirement

Police officers, like all those who might face genuine tactical confrontations, demand a great deal from their handguns. Furthermore, the gun has to convince officers within the context of an entire organization, unit, or department. If the weapon has any flaws or inadequacies, they will be found, and generate heated discussion and complaints to the relevant authorities, who might have just spent a huge slab of the annual budget on purchasing the firearms. To add to the issues, the police officers may have been called upon to fire the gun in public and to take a life with it. Such events, generally speaking, attract intense media interest and investigation, during which the handgun used can be scrutinized and evaluated with forensic diligence, not always in an informed and dispassionate manner. Pity the individuals who have to select new firearms for any police unit.

Before looking at the specific rise and use of the Glock in law-enforcement circles, it is worth clarifying what law-enforcement officers generally look for in a handgun, as the criteria are more complex than might be appreciated. First, some obvious suspects. For reasons already explained, reliability sits at the top of the tree. A handgun in police hands must demonstrate absolutely reliable functioning year after year, through all the seasonal weathers, after thousands of training rounds have been put through the barrel and after the constant knocks of being worn daily. Failures to feed, fire, or eject can happen with almost every firearm, but they must be rare occurrences indeed for a law-enforcement gun.

On par with reliability is the issue of effectiveness. The service handgun has to do its job, namely putting rounds into a target both accurately and with a power sufficient enough to stop an assailant decisively. Here we get into all the wrangles about caliber and power already discussed in previous chapters. At the same time the gun needs to be safe. By this we mean a gun that is both safe to holster and safe to handle. The weapon must be configured to protect against accidental discharge, whether when slipping into a holster or when actually drawn in earnest. So safety mechanisms

ABOVE: A police officer in Vienna, 1986, demonstrates the force's latest acquisition—the G17.

FACING PAGE: A British policewoman armed with Heckler & Koch G36, a Taser, and a G17 pistol stands guard near the scene of a violent incident, 2005.

must be easy to use and absolutely secure, but they must also not interfere with the rapid deployment of the weapon when it came time to shoot. Note that the average time for an armed encounter to play out between police and criminals is 3.5 seconds—there is no time for any complicated physical actions.

Other physical factors are relevant. Weight, for example—no police officer wants to carry an excessively heavy gun around all day—and it must feel comfortable in the hand, and intuitive to handle. One of the biggest considerations, however, is cost. Although police officers can spend whatever they like, or can afford, on personal back-up weapons (if they are allowed to carry such guns), police forces and departments have to purchase large numbers of firearms within a specified budget. The ammunition must also be cheap to purchase. Yet the budget allocation to a firearm is not just about the physical components. For example, the caliber of the gun can affect the duration of training times, with heavier calibers generally requiring lengthier, and therefore more costly, training time than lighter calibers. Thus the decision to purchase a new gun is a complex equation of physical, monetary, and personnel issues. One of the reasons why the Glock has been so successful is that it balances this equation better than many other firearms.

The International Glock

To give this chapter a clear focus, we will study in depth the proliferation of the Glock within the US market from the 1980s to the present day. There are several reasons for this focus. The first is that the United States is one of the world's largest markets for law-enforcement handguns, with the best part of 900,000 officers of various types in active service. The second is that the controversies that accompanied the Glock's progressive adoption by so many police forces in that country actually serve to underline the value of the Glock as a law-enforcement weapon. For as we shall see, there was trenchant opposition to the Glock from various influential quarters, but over time every basic objection was shown to be essentially unwarranted.

Yet away from the United States, we could pick numerous countries around the world that have in whole or part made the shift to the Glock for their frontline officers. As discussed earlier, adoptions of the Glock by police and military units began almost as soon as the gun hit the market in the mid 1980s. If we run the story through to the present day, we see a colorful spectrum of law-enforcement agencies who have taken up the Glock.

They include (see table opposite):

BELOW: An officer of Toronto's Emergency Task Force trains with a G17 equipped with a taclight.

COUNTRY	AGENCY
Australia	New South Wales Department of Corrective Services
	New South Wales Police
	Queensland Police
	Western Australia Police
	Northern Territory Police
Austria	Austrian Federal Police
Brazil	Federal Police Department
Canada	Calgary Police Service
	Edmonton Police Service
	Saskatoon Police Service
	Saskatchewan Police Service
	Toronto Police Service
	Quebec Provincial Police
Ecuador	National Police
Germany	GSG 9
Iceland	Icelandic National Police
Iraq	Iraqi Ministry of Interior police forces
Lithuania	Lithuanian Police
Malaysia	Royal Malaysian Police
	Royal Malaysian Custom
New Zealand	New Zealand Police
Philippines	Philippines National Police
	National Bureau of Investigation
	National Intelligence Coordinating Agency
	Philippine Drug Enforcement Agency
Poland	Polish Police Force
Singapore	Singapore Prison Service
Thailand	Thai National Police
United Kingdom	Specialist Firearms Command of the London Metropolitan Police Service
	Scottish Police Specialist Firearms Units
	Police Service of Northern Ireland

The list of countries here, and the list of agencies within those countries, is by no means exhaustive. What it demonstrates is not only the Glock's commercial success, but also the fact that to achieve adoption it has undergone and passed the huge levels of scrutiny applied to authorize a new state or force firearm.

ABOVE: An international group of police officers train Iraqi officers in Glock handling.

Glock in Iraq

There are some countries that deserve a special mention for their relationship to the Glock. Iraq is a case in point. In the aftermath of the invasion of Iraq by US forces in 2003, a major objective was the re-establishment of the Iraqi police and security forces to maintain law and order. This meant equipping them with standardized firearms, rather than the mish-mash of assorted weapons with which the country was blighted. The US Department of Defense, through the Joint Contracting Command—Iraq/Afghanistan (JCC—I/A), set about purchasing huge volumes of Glock 19 pistols under open-ended indefinite delivery/indefinite quantity (ID/IQ) contracts. (At first the specification issued by the Iraqi Security Ministries was for the G17, but this was discovered to be erroneous and the G19 became the pistol of choice.)

The choice of the Glock raised eyebrows within the US government and among some US firearms manufacturers. The Glock had largely been chosen on a non-competitive basis, but the experience of its proven law-enforcement and military use meant that competitive trials appeared scarcely necessary. The numbers of Glocks in Iraq to date are unclear, but they certainly number more than 139,000 (a figure reported in 2007). The distribution to the police officers was commented upon in the following American Forces Press Service release in 2004:

Iraqi Police Service to Graduate Largest Class Ever

"WASHINGTON, Oct. 10, 2004—The Iraqi Police Service will graduate 1,137 police recruits from a police basic training course at the Jordan International Police Training Center in Amman, Jordan, Oct. 14, a Multinational Force Iraq news release said.

It is the single largest graduation of Iraqi officers from the basic training course. Since establishing the formal training requirements for police recruits at the center, approximately 5,700 officers have completed training at the school.

The eight-week training program—divided into general policing and operational policing components—runs recruits through intensive basic police education in modern methods, the release said.

Instructors from the Multinational Security Transition Command's Civilian Police Assistance Training Team come from 16 different countries including the United States. The team is tasked with assisting the Iraqi government to train, mentor, and equip its civil security forces.

The graduating officers will return for duty in Iraq in various assignments throughout the country.

The Multinational Security Transition Command-Iraq also delivered 10,000 9mm Glock pistols to the Baghdad Public Service Academy Oct. 9 for distribution to Iraqi Police Service recruits attending the school, a second MNF-I release said.

The delivery is just part of the overall distribution of nearly 41,000 Glocks earmarked for Iraqi Police Service officers received in country by the multinational command two weeks ago.

In addition to the Oct. 9 issue, a 10,000-plus Glock shipment went out to Iraqi Police Service advisors in the various major support commands for issue to officers already in service throughout the country.

The two distributions raise the total Glocks delivered in the past week to more than 20,000 pistols, according to the release. The Multinational Security Transition Command-Iraq's Civilian Police Assistance Training Team will distribute the remaining 20,000 weapons in the coming weeks."

ABOVE: The G19 has become one of the most popular models of law enforcement gun, suited to a greater variety of hand sizes than the G17.

ABOVE: **A US Army
instructor trains an Iraqi
police recruit in handling
the G19, demonstrating
mag reloads.**

The article is noteworthy if only for the rate at which the Glock has been
flowing into Iraq, at one point some 20,000 pistols in just a week. Yet the
widespread distribution of the Glock makes sense. Only when a single type
of handgun is common to most officers in a force can that force develop
standardized training and tactical procedures, understood by the majority
of officers.

Philippines

Another country that has understood this message, plus appreciated the
Glock's qualities, is the Philippines. In mid 2014, the country hit the
world's headlines by making the largest ever single purchase of Glocks
in history—74,000 G17 Gen4 handguns, all of them destined for the
Philippine National Police (PNP). Prior to this acquisition, the Glock
already had a presence in the country, it being used by the likes of the elite

Special Action Force (SAF)—a counter-terrorism unit within the PNP—plus the officers of the National Bureau of Investigation (NBI). Yet this did not mean that the Glock was simply accepted into service without question. The PNP first assessed the performance feedback on data on the Glock from worldwide law-enforcement and military forces, plus evaluated Glock's ability to supply the guns on time and to budget. Next, Glock handguns were put through some intensive test firings. For example, one production handgun was put through a four-day, 20,000 rounds firing trial, without significant problems or stoppages. Thus the Glock has been taken with confidence into the Philippines.

As these examples show, just two of many, the Glock is continually expanding its international law-enforcement customer base. Now we turn back to the example of the United States for a more in-depth look at how the gun came to dominate the largest police market in the world.

ABOVE: Police officers in the Philippines show off their newly received G17 pistols during a ceremony in Manila, July 2013.

FACING PAGE: The belt kit of this US police officer includes a Glock, plus two spare magazines in a ready pouch at the front.

The Glock in the United States

The world of police handguns in the immediate decades after World War II was dominated by one particular type—the revolver. The revolver had been serving US police officers well since the days of the Wild West, and its format and performance was thoroughly engrained into the culture and mindset of American law enforcement.

If we scroll forward to the present day, we find extremely few police officers still using revolvers as their primary weapon. (It is more common to carry revolvers as secondary back-up firearms, although even this usage has been eroded by compact pistols.) As just one example of the decline of revolver use, the New York Police Department was carrying 30,000 revolvers in 1993, and just 2,000 in 2004. Doubtless the figures for revolver-carrying today are even fewer.

So what changed? For a start, during the 1950s and 1960s semi-automatic handguns became more prevalent on the world's market, especially from producers in Western and Eastern Europe and from the Soviet Union. This factor, plus the tactical and ammunition-capacity advantages of the pistol, led to more worldwide military organizations finally abandoning their revolvers in favor of pistols. Ironically, the United States had already taken this step with the military adoption of the M1911 earlier in the century, but this changed did not percolate quickly out to the police.

One outcome of the generally widening distribution of pistols, however, was that the police increasingly began to come up against them in street engagements. An abiding theme in the development of the US law enforcement armory throughout history is the synergy between criminal and police firepower. Dating back to the Prohibition era, the US police service has fought a kind of arms race at street level, increasing its own firepower to match that of the criminals.

During the 1950s and 1960s, thus began what has been called the "militarization" of the US police, with increasing acquisition of military-grade weaponry to combat the criminal acquisition of high-capacity, semi-auto handguns, submachine guns, and assault rifles. There is much debate about whether the level of threat is perceived or real, and whether the tactical training that police today receive is entirely appropriate for the reality of policing. However, one fact was certain during this period: criminals could, on occasions, outgun the police, especially police armed with nothing more than a six-shooter.

Change was coming, but it was slow, as the revolver culture had as much a psychological hold as a practical and financial one. The first force to make the move was the Illinois State Police in 1968, when it converted from its revolvers to the Smith & Wesson Model 39. Slowly others began to follow suit, but it wasn't really until the 1980s that the pace began to pick up and more departments began to make the switch. Yet still the revolver prevailed in large numbers.

FACING PAGE: Police and Drug Enforcement Agency (DEA) officials draw their Glocks. The DEA utilizes the G22, G23, and G27 models.

Miami Shooting

It would take a tragic event to raise consciousness about the need to upgun to the police, and some experiences were nationally formative in terms of how the police looked at the future of police firearms. On April 11, 1986, eight FBI agents, supported by officers of the Miami Metro-Dade PD, were conducting a patrol of an area in southwest Miami, on the lookout for a suspicious vehicle—specifically a black Chevrolet Monte Carlo with a Florida license plate. There had been several violent bank and security vehicle robberies in the area over the previous months, resulting in the death of one guard and the wounding of several others, and the vehicle was on their wanted list. At around 9.30am, they spotted it, occupied by two brutal criminals: William Russell Matix and Michael Platt, both former US Army soldiers. They were also heavily armed: a 12-gauge shotgun, a Remington Mini-14 .223 (5.66mm) carbine, and two Smith & Wesson .357 Magnum revolvers.

BELOW: Glock is not the only manufacturer offering innovative law-enforcement handguns. Here is the sub-compact Springfield XD, which can hold 13 + 1 rounds of 9mm or 12 +1 of .40 S&W.

The FBI team opted to pull over the car and make a felony arrest. Three FBI vehicles, occupied by Special Agents Benjamin Grogan/Gerald Dove, Richard Manauzzi/ Gordan McNeill, and John Hanlon/Edmundo Mireles, rammed the Monte Carlo and forced it off the road, the primary FBI vehicle relying on the back-up of another FBI car positioned a short distance away, holding two more officers. The criminals' vehicle was rammed against a tree and came to a stop, but Platt unleashed a volley of 13 shots from his Mini-14 from the passenger seat, followed by a blast from Matix's 12-gauge shotgun.

It was the beginning of a bloodbath. Special Agent Gordon McNeill was hit in the hand by a .223 round, and Mireles took a round in the forearm. The officers returned fire, and at this point Matix was hit in the right forearm. He fell back into the car, and was then hit by an FBI pistol round in the side of the head, rendering him unconscious before yet another bullet slammed into him, striking his neck and moving down into his chest. He began the slow journey toward death. Platt, meanwhile, exited the car holding his Mini-14, and charged the police officers, attempting to capture one of the FBI vehicles (his own car was trapped between two of the FBI cars). On the way, he took no fewer than six hits from the FBI guns, but he still made it to the vehicle, where he then killed Special Agents Dove and Grogan and shot Special Agent Hanlon in the hand and pelvis.

So far, two FBI agents were dead and three were seriously injured. But it was not over yet. Matix regained consciousness and crawled over to join Platt in the police cruiser. Now Mireles, despite severe injuries, managed to operate and empty his shotgun with one hand and, miraculously, hit both men, stopping them from driving off. Platt, still fighting, exited the vehicle and went over to Mireles. He fired three shots at the officer but missed, then he returned to the car. It was a fatal mistake. Mireles got to his feet, pulled out his .357 revolver, and moved over to the car—he shot Platt and Matix repeatedly at close range, finally killing them.

Shift to Semi-autos

The Miami shootout shocked the FBI to the core. How had two criminals caused death and injury despite being outnumbered 4:1? Critically, the two criminals, who were not fuelled by drugs or alcohol, had been hit a total of 18 times, and the first bullet that hit Platt inflicted a fatal wound. Yet the penetration and damage caused by the police bullets had not been sufficient for a decisive take-down early on, plus those officers using .357 service revolvers had been hampered by slow reloading times. These factors led the FBI to adopt a wider range of auto handguns and also the powerful 10mm Auto Smith & Wesson 1076. The 10mm round certainly packed the requisite punch, but when fired it kicked like a mule and hence reduced the accuracy of rapid fire and made the gun hard to handle in less resilient hands.

Consequently, the FBI gradually transitioned to a less powerful .40 Smith & Wesson cartridge. The FBI experience, and its shift to semi-auto handguns, was not lost on the rest of the country. Nor was the wider United

ABOVE: **An FBI instructor demonstrates an Interactive Firearms Training System, a live-action screen-based system hooked up to this G17 training weapon.**

States shielded from the realities of escalating gun violence. In 1979, the total number of firearms homicides in the country was 13,582. In 1980, that number had leapt to 14,377, and over the next 20 years the figures just seemed to climb—15,025 in 1990, 16,376 in 1991, 17,083 in 1993 (the peak year). In cities like New York, Los Angeles, Chicago, and Philadelphia the violence reached the level of a small war.

It was into this context that the police forces of the United States decided to pack more holstered firepower. The most popular handgun models were from Beretta, Smith & Wesson, Sig Sauer, and above all, Glock. The Glock began to make sales to law-enforcement agencies from March 1986, albeit with relatively small sales to departments in Kansas, Florida, and Minnesota. But the game-changing contract came in May 1987, with the Miami Police Department. In 1986, following some soul-searching about the department's handguns, the decision was made to switch to a 9mm double-action pistol. Following tests on several other brands of handgun, in 1987 the department began a small-scale trial of the Glock 17. The gun was truly tested to destruction. Kasler remarks:

"One test included throwing and dropping a loaded (primed case only) Model 17 numerous time on steel and concrete from distance of up to 60 feet [18m]. Another fully loaded (with real ammunition) Model 17 was submerged in saltwater for fifty

hours, then retrieved and discharged; it fired flawlessly. Then the same pistol was reloaded and left exposed to the air for two days but, upon firing, malfunctioned after the first round fired. Upon inspection it was determined that some corrosion had formed inside the weapon that had interfered with slide cycling. The pistol was unloaded, swished in a bucket of kerosene, and reloaded; it then fired flawlessly. One of Miami's final tests of the Glock 17 was to fire 1,000 rounds of Winchester Silvertip ammunition in forty-five minutes; all rounds were fired with no malfunction."

—Kasler, 1992, p.30

The trial was utterly convincing, and in the autumn of 1987 the entire Miami PD switched to the G17 as its standard handgun.

Controversy and Questions

After the Miami adoption, the Glock began its inexorable rise to becoming America's number one police gun. More and more departments tested out the pistol, and were convinced that with its three safety features, reliability, and high-capacity magazine the Glock would balance out the apparent increase in criminal firepower. By 1992, the gun was in the hands of 250,000 officers in 4,500 of the nation's 13,000 police departments.

Yet the movement toward the Glock was resisted significantly from many quarters. The criticisms focused particularly on the lack of an external safety device, which it was claimed resulted in a high accidental-discharge rate. Glock did respond to some of these concerns. For example, the Metro Dade Police Department wanted to adopt the Glock, but felt that the trigger pull was a little on the light side given the lack of safety switch. Glock responded by changing the angle of the connector ramp from 90 degrees to 105 degrees, thus increasing the trigger pull to 8 pounds (3.6kg) instead of 5 pounds (2.3kg).

Some adaptations were also required to prompt the New York Police Department (NYPD) to move to the Glock. The force began testing 200 G17s in 1986, and in 1994 the G19 Gen2 made it onto the official list of the guns offered to officers—today about 72 percent of the NYPD's officers use the Glock as their primary handgun. However, there was concern that the trigger pull was too light, and needed increasing to prevent officers on the street from unleashing too many rounds from their high-capacity magazines. Actually, the trigger pull was already 8 pounds (3.6kg), due to modifications made to the trigger spring for the New York State Police. In these modifications, producing what is aptly called the "New York Trigger," the coil-spring mechanism was replaced by a sprung polymer fitting that pressed directly on the underside of the sear plate, increasing the trigger pull to 8 pounds (3.6kg). This model of New York Trigger is known as the NY1. The NYPD, however, required something even stronger, so the NY2 model ramped up the trigger-spring configuration to produce up to a whopping 11 pounds (5 kg) of pull. Although the NY2 was naturally a step in the direction of safety, it has not been popular with the officers. The increase in trigger pull, it is claimed, reduces shot accuracy and thereby causes danger to innocent bystanders. We will not unpack the complexities of the debate here, but suffice to say that the New York Trigger has still not prevented the Glock from becoming the dominant handgun in this enormous police department.

Looking through the US press reports of the 1990s, which gave a lot of attention to the Glock, accidental discharges do seem to have been something of a problem with the introduction of the fast-firing gun from Austria. For example, the Washington, DC, Metropolitan Police Department adopted the Glock in the late 1980s. In the decade following the adoption,

BELOW: A 30-round 9mm clip for a G19. Although giving a hefty firepower boost, the extended mags create very heavy loaded weapons.

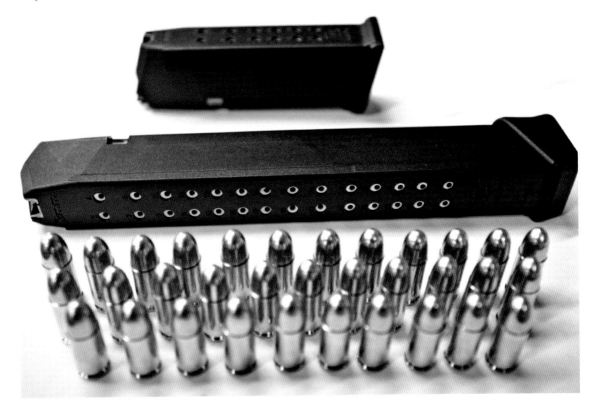

there were a total of 120 Glock accidental discharges, and in 1996 alone the city paid out over $1.4 million in costs related to these discharges. A special report into the subject was presented by the *Washington Post* in 1998, and it listed many of the discharge incidents. Some are almost comical. One female officer was unloading her gun at home, when her husband accidentally bumped into her, resulting in the officer shooting herself in the foot. Another officer put a bullet through the floor of her own apartment, hitting the resident below in the leg. A large number of officers shot themselves in the thigh or leg while holstering or unholstering the gun. Other incidents are far darker. On October 10, 1989, a police officer's two-year-old daughter was killed after she accidentally shot herself in the head with her father's pistol, one of a handful of children killed or injured with their parent's firearm. Guns went off several times during routine arrests or traffic stops, sometimes with fatal consequences.

The frequency of the discharges and the high profile of some cases gave the press much adverse ammunition to fire against the Glock. Furthermore, many high-ranking police officers were also concerned. In 1991/92, for example, the Chicago Police Department actually voted against adopting the Glock, branding the weapon as too dangerous for general use (although they did authorize four other brands of semi-auto handgun for adoption).

GLOCK 19 GEN2
DATE:
1988
CALIBER:
9 x 19mm
WEIGHT (EMPTY):
23.6oz (670g)
LENGTH:
7.3in (187mm)
BARREL LENGTH:
4.01in (102mm)
MAGAZINE CAPACITY
(STANDARD):
15
EFFECTIVE RANGE:
50yds (45.72m)

RIGHT: The 9mm Glock 19 is now the weapon of choice for many police departments in the US, including Washington, D.C., New York, Chicago, Los Angeles, Philadelphia, and Houston.

In reality, most of the problems with the Glock seemed to be due to much needed catch-up in the officer training program, rather than to any inherent flaw in the weapon design. The *Washington Post* investigation found that "75 percent of all DC officers involved in shootings during 1996 failed to comply with the retraining regulation. One officer waited so long to come to the range that firearms instructors found a spider nest growing inside his Glock." Indeed, when studying the lists of accidental discharges in more detail, we do find that many of them are caused by activities that would result in other brands of handgun going off accidentally—stuffing the gun into waistbelts; reholstering with the finger still on the trigger; holding the gun while attempting to handcuff a suspect at the same time. On the plus side, in a firefight the Glock had the rapid-fire capacity required to put down an assailant in the least space of time, and those officers who did have to draw the gun in earnest generally praised its performance.

Mechanical Issues

Another form of resistance to the Glock came from those who claimed that the gun simply wasn't reliable enough, when trialed against other (usually US-branded) firearms. This accusation is curious, given what we have already seen regarding the Glock's impressive durability.

One particularly prominent example of this take on things came from the California Highway Patrol (CHP) in the late 1980s and early 1990s. (See Kasler for the full discussion of this episode.) Like many other police departments, the CHP began to review its handgun policy, and in 1989 focused on comparing 10mm (0.393in) semi-auto pistols against the other calibers that the CHP used. The investigation was warm toward the idea of using .40 (which the CHP referred to as "10mm Short") or 10mm handguns, and a total of eight different models of gun were tested, including the 10mm G20 and the .40 G22 and G23. There was also one gun from Colt (10mm Double Eagle). All other guns evaluated were from Smith & Wesson.

Reading the report, the responses to the Glock guns are particularly adverse, so much so that it is worth quoting some passages at length:

"Glock Model 20, 10 Millimeter

The Glock 20 10mm was returned to the factory immediately after its arrival due to excessive clearance found between extractor and bolt face causing it to malfunction during the initial inspection test firing. It was returned with the

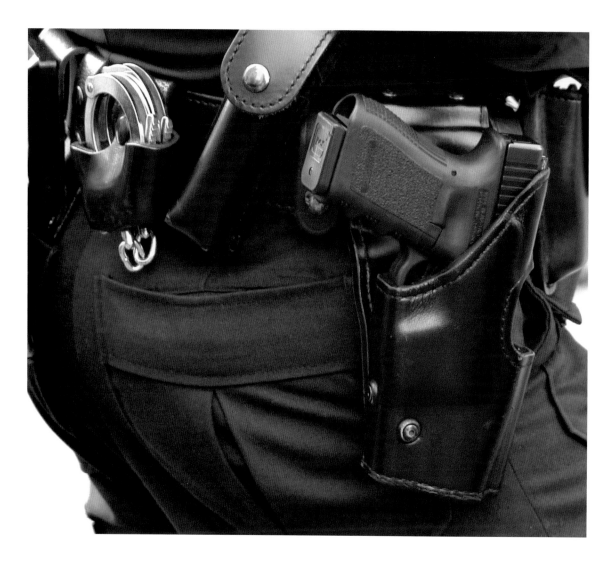

ABOVE: This New York Police Department (NYPD) officer carries a G19, officially adopted in 1994.

problem corrected on March 15 and its testing was resumed. The Glock was the only weapon submitted for testing that had no hammer. All the Glock's firing mechanisms other than the trigger are contained inside the weapon's slide and grip frame. During the evaluation of the weapon design characteristics, it was noted that the magazine, whether loaded or empty, had to be physically extracted from the grip frame, never dropping free. The magazine follower also bound frequently inside the magazine body, occasionally causing difficulty loading, in some instances even preventing the loading of the magazine to its capacity. Later in the testing, the follower also worked its way completely out through the top of the magazine past the feed lips. The Glock 20 exhibited the strongest recoil of all 10mm pistols tested. This made it the most difficult of all weapons to control when firing multiple shot groups. When it was fired by trainees who were being observed by the test staff, the consensus of opinion was that the recoil was excessive for officers of smaller stature and hand size.

During the endurance firing, some 205 malfunctions were experienced with the Glock 20. The magazines always had to be removed from the weapon by hand, failing to drop free on their own. The malfunction rate for the Glock 20 was calculated to be one in every 19 rounds. Firing was halted at approximately 3,800 rounds because of severe cracking and deterioration of the bolt face at the firing pin opening, which caused repeated malfunctions. Additionally, upon final inspection of the weapon, cracks were found in the plastic frame rails adjacent to the magazine well at the rear of the barrel locking lug.

Glock Model 22, 10 Millimeter Short (.40 S&W)

Two Glock #22 weapons were involved in this testing. The first suffered a barrel rupture due to a defective bullet fired during endurance testing. Subsequently a second weapon was provided and subjected to the entire test battery.

As with the Glock #20, the magazine had to be manually removed from the grip frame of the weapon during each magazine change. The recoil generated by the Glock #22 when firing was second only to the smaller framed Glock #23. This recoil was found to be difficult to control when multiple shot groups were fired. When small-handed shooters fired the weapon, they all indicated that the recoil caused difficulty in control. The endurance test was completed with 37 recorded

BELOW: A 10mm G20, the price tag giving a good idea of the how affordable a Glock can be.

RIGHT: A G22 in disassembled state. With its powerful .40-cal round, the G22 has become a popular law-enforcement choice.

RIGHT: A G22 in disassembled state. With its powerful .40-cal round, the G22 has become a popular law-enforcement choice.

malfunctions, which resulted in a malfunction rate of one in every 137 rounds fired.

The weapon was cleaned and allowed to cool on four occasions due to malfunctions occurring from debris buildup. Upon completion of the test, the weapon was inspected by the academy gunsmiths. During this inspection, cracks were found in the plastic frame rails adjacent to the magazine well at the rear of the barrel block.

Glock Model 23, 10 Millimeter Short (.40 S&W)

The Glock #23 was the lightest and smallest of all pistols tested. It, like the other Glocks, would not allow the magazine to drop free when released. The magazine follower could also be twisted and bound inside the magazine. Recoil from the Glock #23 was substantially higher than any other 10mm Short (.40 S&W) weapon fired. The endurance testing of the Glock was halted at 1,038 rounds due to the breakage of the trigger spring rendering it incapable of continuing. To this point in the test, the Glock #23 has a malfunction rate of one in 25, experiencing 41 total malfunctions. Just as was found on the other Glock test weapons, the

GLOCK 22 GEN4
DATE:
2010
CALIBER:
.40
WEIGHT (EMPTY):
25.59oz (725g)
LENGTH:
7.95in (202mm)
BARREL LENGTH:
4.49in (114mm)
MAGAZINE CAPACITY
(STANDARD):
15
EFFECTIVE RANGE:
55yds (50m)

plastic frame was cracked adjacent to the magazine well behind the barrel locking block on the Glock #23. This was discovered during a final inspection of the weapon."

—CHP, *Test and Evaluation: 10mm Semi-Automatic Pistol*, May 1990)

It would be hard to create a more adverse assessment of the Glock pistols. According to the report's conclusions, the Glock appears to be profoundly unreliable at almost every level of functionality, with the added tactical concern of its non-drop magazines.

GLOCK 23
DATE:
2010
CALIBER:
.40 S&W
WEIGHT (EMPTY):
23.65oz (670g)
LENGTH:
7.36in (187mm)
BARREL LENGTH:
4.01in (102mm)
MAGAZINE CAPACITY
(STANDARD):
13
EFFECTIVE RANGE:
55yds (50m)

RIGHT: The LAPD has
also bought into the Glock,
particularly in .40 and
.45 calibers.

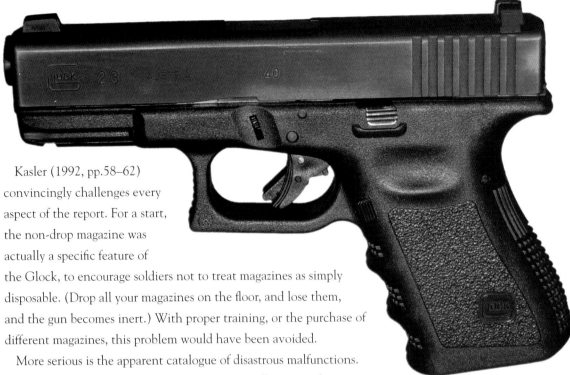

Kasler (1992, pp.58–62) convincingly challenges every aspect of the report. For a start, the non-drop magazine was actually a specific feature of the Glock, to encourage soldiers not to treat magazines as simply disposable. (Drop all your magazines on the floor, and lose them, and the gun becomes inert.) With proper training, or the purchase of different magazines, this problem would have been avoided.

More serious is the apparent catalogue of disastrous malfunctions. However, the guns used in the testing were actually pre-production samples, which specifically weren't intended for the arduous testing conditions. Many of the problems cited, such as frame cracks, would not have happened in production versions of the guns. Furthermore, it is unclear just how many of the general stoppages were down to either the ammunition or the user. As we saw in the previous chapter, the incorrect grip (all too easy to apply to an unfamiliar firearm) can cause stoppages in the Glock, as can ammunition that doesn't quite meet the performance requirements. Given the astonishing reliability of the Glock in other tests—think of the Miami PD trials outlined above—it scarcely seems plausible that had the CHP been issued with standard production guns for the trials, then the problems encountered would have remained the same. As it turned out, the CHP opted for the Smith & Wesson 4006.

Other US police departments, such as the Scottsdale PD (Arizona), also tested the Glock at the same time and with direct reference to the CHP report. At Scottsdale, a G22 was put through a 5,000-round endurance firing. The conclusions couldn't have been more different:

"Of the 5,000 rounds, three were found to be defective and replaced. Three operator-induced malfunctions were experienced during the testing. On

GLOCK 23 GEN3
DATE:
1996
CALIBER:
.40
WEIGHT (EMPTY):
21.16oz (600g)
LENGTH:
6.85in (174mm)
BARREL LENGTH:
4.02in (102mm)
MAGAZINE CAPACITY
(STANDARD):
13
EFFECTIVE RANGE:
50yds (45.7m)

FACING PAGE: **This plain-clothes officer in New York supplements his Glock with a non-lethal Taser option.**

these occasions the officer allowed his thumb to ride up the frame and trip the slide stop level, which engaged the slide and locked it in the rear position, which is what the lever is meant to do. This is a training issue and will be addressed at that time. It should be noted that this only occurred after the officer had fired several magazines and was feeling fatigued.

No feeding, extracting, or ejecting malfunctions were experienced throughout the testing.

The inspection revealed what would be considered less than normal wear to a pistol."

(Quoted in Kasler, 1992, p.67)

The Scottsdale evaluation is at a polar opposite to that produced by the CHP, and crucially makes allowance for operator error and the need for appropriate training. Such is true of any handgun, or indeed any firearm, if it is to perform as it is meant to.

Glock Trends

Despite the controversies in the press, and the resistance from some police departments, there was no stopping the spread of the Glock, which by the end of 2010 was the US law-enforcement community's most common handgun. Throughout this period, Glock was expanding its range, enabling it to keep pace with the various trends and preferences emerging.

One of the key developments was the shift, during the 1990s, to larger-caliber handguns, generally of .40 or .45 size. A huge amount of research into terminal ballistics had been conducted during the Vietnam War, and this prompted much investigation into the ideal caliber for self-defense. We have already looked at wounding mechanisms of ammunition in an earlier chapter, and seen how the right choice of handgun caliber is not necessarily solved by the science. But in the 1990s, it was felt by many that the 9mm was a little too underpowered to deliver the "stopping power" required on the street. Actually, there was also confusion between "stopping power" and "knock-down power." The former is a legitimate concept, and refers to the capacity of the ammunition to inflict a wound that will eventually stop an assailant from being able to deliver aggressive action. It should be noted that one bullet on its own rarely achieves this goal, which is why police officers generally fire many times and keep firing until the victim is on the floor. To the general public, this often appears as excessive force.

"Knock-down power," however, is a myth. It is the idea that a bullet can be so powerful that it literally throws the opponent to the ground through kinetic energy. For various physical reasons, this is nonsense except in long-arm weapons of truly formidable power, such as a 20mm (0.787in) cannon. According to the laws of physics, every reaction has an equal and opposite

LEFT: Indianapolis police updated their G22s to the Gen3 version of the same model in 2008.

reaction, and the gun that is strong enough to hurl a human onto his back would also deliver enough recoil to do the same to the shooter. To debunk such myths, some firearms experts have gone to the lengths of standing on one leg while wearing heavy-duty body armor, and allowing themselves to be shot with 7.62 x 51mm NATO rifle rounds. Although some wobbling

RIGHT: Apart from options for SWAT team members, extended Glock magazines are never used in regular police work.

was involved, they generally managed to stay standing on one leg.

Regardless of the levels of understanding about stopping power, the general movement since the 1990s has been toward the .40 Glocks and the .45 Glocks. For example, in August 2007 the Sandy Springs (GA) Police Department switched to the G21 SF, in .45 Auto, while the Los Angeles Police Department (LAPD) includes, among its admittedly wide range of handgun types, the .40 G22, G23, and G27 and the .45 G21, G30, and G36.

At the same time, there are reports suggesting that a swing back to 9mm might be taking place, with some police departments swapping their .40 and .45 Glocks back to 9mm weapons. Partly this is because of training and cost issues—9mm ammunition is extremely cheap, plus you don't need to use so much of it to bring a novice up to a qualified status. There is also the fact that while some cartridges are still better than others, shot placement remains king in terms of stopping power. Finally, while the .40s and .45s of the 1990s offered superior power to the 9mm, the gap has been closing. Continual improvements in cartridge and bullet design and powder formulations have upped both the velocity and penetration of the humble 9mm, meaning that the rationale behind the .40 and .45 is not quite as strong. This perspective is reflected in recent documents produced by the FBI, which justify a swing back toward the traditional 9mm round.

The FBI document defiantly asserts the qualities of the 9mm. According to its view, the round offers all the penetration, mag capacity, and ballistics required for a serviceable combat cartridge, with the heavier cartridges offering little discernible advantage when compared with modern high-performance 9mm brands. One particularly interesting admission is that in an engagement officers can miss with 70–80 percent of the rounds fired. This acknowledgement is used to reinforce the point that accuracy improves when firing the smaller-caliber round.

GLOCK 30

DATE:
1997
CALIBER:
.45 Auto
LENGTH:
6.96in (177mm)
BARREL LENGTH:
3.78in (96mm)
WEIGHT (LOADED):
33.89oz (960g)
MAGAZINE CAPACITY
(STANDARD):
10
RANGE:
50yds (45.72m)

Another general trend in law enforcement that Glock has embraced is the growing demand for tactical accessories. This trend takes its place in the "militarization" of the police mentioned earlier. Back in 1967, the LAPD's Inspector Daryl Gates formed the country's first Special Weapons and Tactics Unit (SWAT), which was trained and armed to handle high-risk

BELOW: A disassembled G30, showing the diminutive 3.77-inch (96 mm) barrel.

FBI TRAINING DIVISION:
FBI ACADEMY, QUANTICO, VA

Executive Summary of Justification for Law Enforcement Partners

• Caliber debates have existed in law enforcement for decades.

• Most of what is "common knowledge" with ammunition and its effects on the human target are rooted in myth and folklore.

• Projectiles are what ultimately wound our adversaries and the projectile needs to be the basis for the discussion on what caliber is best.

• In all the major law enforcement calibers there exist projectiles which have a high likelihood of failing LEOs [Law Enforcement Officers] in a shooting incident and there are projectiles which have a high incident likelihood of succeeding for LEOs in a shooting incident.

• Handgun stopping power is simply a myth.

• The single most important factor in effectively wounding a human target is to have penetration to a scientifically valid depth (FBI uses 12–18").

• LEOs miss between 70–80 percent of the shots fired during a shooting incident.

• Contemporary projectiles (since 2007) have dramatically increased the terminal effectiveness of many premium line law enforcement projectiles (emphasis on the 9mm Luger offerings).

• 9mm Luger now offers select projectiles which are, under identical testing conditions, outperforming most of the premium line .40 S&W and .45 Auto projectiles tested by the FBI.

• 9mm Luger offers higher magazine capacities, less recoil, lower cost (both in ammunition and wear on the weapons) and higher functional reliability rates (in FBI weapons).

• The majority of FBI shooters are both FASTER in shot strings fired and more ACCURATE with shooting a 9mm Luger vs. shooting a .40 S&W (similar sized weapons).

• There is little to no noticeable difference in the wound tracks between premium line law Auto enforcement projectiles from 9mm Luger through the .45 Auto.

• Given contemporary bullet construction, LEO's can field (with proper bullet selection) 9mm Lugers with all of the terminal performance potential of any other law enforcement pistol caliber with none of the disadvantages present with the "larger" calibers.

(FBI Training Division, 2014)

FACING PAGE: An Indian Special Protection Group (SPG) officer. He is armed with a FN F2000 assault rifle and carries a G17 in a side holster.

violent encounters and hostage-rescue situations, ones that the regular police
officers couldn't take on. The concept of the SWAT team spread throughout
the United States, so that virtually every police department today has a
tactically enhanced group of officers, with heavier firepower.

The Glock has itself been very popular with SWAT-style teams, for all
the reasons we have explored in this book. Furthermore, the addition of the
accessory rail on the Gen3 models meant that the tactical capabilities of
an already effective handgun can be enhanced further. SWAT team tactics,

LEFT: Anaheim, California. A police officer teaches a local resident about the principles of handling a G22 during a police Citizens Academy course.

especially in hostage-rescue situations, can involve cutting the lights within buildings and utilizing smoke, gas, or stun grenades. Thus once inside a hostile building, there might be low visibility, and here an underbarrel light or laser proves useful. Thus Glock accessories have enjoyed strong sales among elite police forces, but, generally, what the specialists buy trickles down to the regular officers. So although the standard holstered pistol will not usually be fitted with a light or laser, increasingly volumes of these accessories are sold to police officers as tactical augmentations.

G33 GEN4
DATE:
2010
CALIBER:
.357 Safe Action
LENGTH:
6.41in (163mm)
BARREL LENGTH:
3.42in (87mm)
WEIGHT (LOADED):
26.65oz (755g)
MAGAZINE CAPACITY
(STANDARD):
9
EFFECTIVE RANGE:
50yds (45.72m)

Criminal Use

Before moving on from the subject of law-enforcement use of Glocks, it would be remiss to avoid acknowledging that Glocks are also weapons of choice for some in the criminal community in the United States, and worldwide. The reference to *Die Hard 2* at the beginning of this chapter shows just how much public consciousness has been attuned to the Glock as a problem as well as a solution. We must be careful here to separate hysteria from fact. Glocks are high-quality weapons sold principally through legitimate channels, their price and quality often prohibiting their distribution among the less-salutary sectors of society. In fact, cheap and small revolvers are by far the most common handguns used in crime, these being a fraction of the cost of a professional pistol, even on the black market. Nevertheless, the Glock, like the Mac 10 and Uzi, has attracted a media interest often disproportionate to its overall impact on society.

On October 16, 1991, in Killeen, Texas, Luby's Café, on 1705 East Central Texas Expressway, was packed with diners, tucking into lunch at this particularly popular haunt. What the approximately 80 people did not know was that violence was heading their way in the form of 35-year-old Texan George Jo Hennard, driving his pick-up truck. In the truck with him were two handguns—a Ruger P89 and a G17. He was also carrying huge amounts of ready-loaded ammunition. At 12.45pm, Hennard drove his truck straight through the front window of the diner, glass exploding over the customers. Then, as the customers recovered from what they thought was a freak automobile accident, he emerged from the cab with his Glock in hand and began shooting.

An awful chaotic scene followed. Reloading his Glock as he ran out of ammunition, and later resorting to the Ruger, Hennard proceeded to shoot as many people as he could in as short a space of time as possible. Over just 12 ghastly minutes, Hennard killed 22 people, wounding many more. Only when he was finally cornered by police did the situation end, with Hennard killing himself with a single shot to the head.

The Killeen massacre provoked the usual soul-searching in the United States, as society and the media traded blows about the pros and cons of gun ownership. The killing also came at a politically sensitive moment, when the US House of Representatives was conducting a long-running debate on gun control. One of the topics for discussion by Congress was the motion to ban high-capacity magazines, a discussion that gained added energy when the terrible news from Killeen arrived. The incident was one of a string of massacres that had plagued the United States over the previous years, and guns like the Glock also came under the same scrutiny as assault rifles and other powerful semi-auto weapons. The media seized upon the Glock's role in the massacre, some arguing that had the gun been fitted with a lower capacity of magazine, more people would remain alive.

BELOW: A first-generation G17 is put through its paces on a police gun range in Virginia.

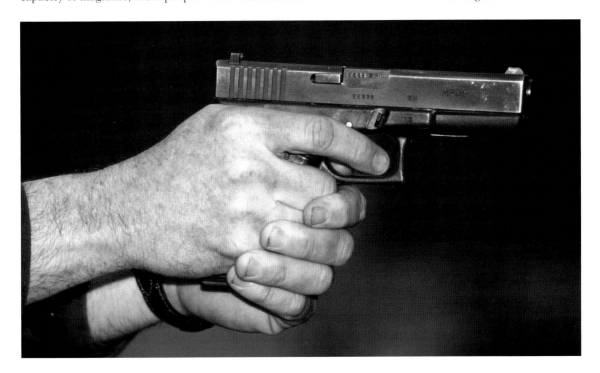

There would be several more years of legal wrangling, and a handful of further major shooting incidents, before, in 1994, the Clinton administration passed the Public Safety and Recreational Firearms Use Protection Act, commonly known as the Federal Assault Weapons Ban (AWB). Although the law was primarily aimed at civilian ownership of weapons such as the Uzi and AK-47, handguns were also implicated through the banning of high-capacity magazines. The bill clarified what it meant by this:

"(31) The term "large capacity ammunition feeding device"—(A) means a magazine, belt, drum, feed strip, or similar device manufactured after the date of enactment of the Violent Crime Control and Law Enforcement Act of 1994 that has a capacity of, or that can be readily restored or converted to accept, more than 10 rounds of ammunition; but (B) does not include an attached tubular device designed to accept, and capable of operating only with .22 caliber rimfire ammunition."

—US Senate and House of Representatives, H.R. 3355, "Violent Crime Control and Law Enforcement Act of 1994," p.204

BELOW: These plastic handguns, modeled after the G23 .40-caliber pistol, were used by students in training given by FBI instructors, 2011.

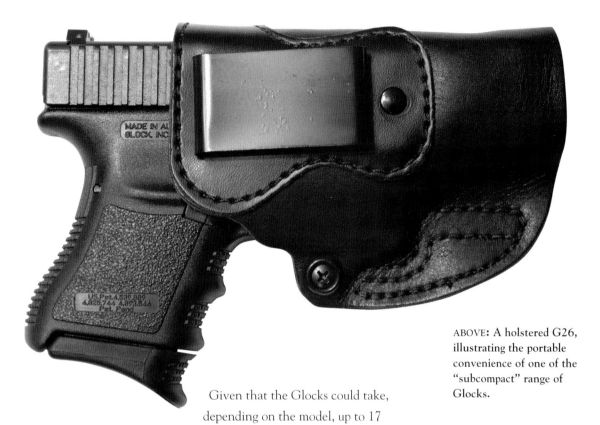

ABOVE: A holstered G26, illustrating the portable convenience of one of the "subcompact" range of Glocks.

Given that the Glocks could take, depending on the model, up to 17 rounds, they were obviously implicated in this bill, which came into force on September 13, 1994. Yet a crucial element of the act was that its regulations only applied to guns or components manufactured after this date, not weapons already in the system. With this in mind, Glock went into overdrive, producing as many guns and high-capacity magazines as it could before the ban came into effect. The demand was enormous, but so was the level of importation into the United States. It ensured that once the ban did come into effect, there was little shortage of Glocks or high-capacity magazines. The act expired on September 13, 2004, with attempts to renew its provisions failing.

If there were a conclusion from this chapter, it would be that the Glock is arguably a near-perfect law-enforcement firearm. The Glock company has certainly been shrewd and persistent in the way it presents its handguns to this market, but commercial acumen alone cannot explain the phenomenon of the weapon's popularity among professionals. Nor does its show signs of abating, either in the United States or among the Glock's dozens of users worldwide. It will take a weapon equally as ground-breaking to unseat the Glock from its position.

The Glock in Military Use

Turning to the Glock as a military pistol, we have to acknowledge from the outset that handguns in general have a very different status in military contexts than in law-enforcement units. One of the biggest contrasts is that handguns are almost never primary weapons in the military—that role is usually taken by the rifle. In fact, considering the panoply of small arms and heavy weaponry possessed by professional military units, it is a wonder that they carry handguns at all.

FACING PAGE: A member of the Malaysian peacekeeping force holds a Glock 19, retrieved from a villager in Dili in June 2006.

In many armies, handgun distribution is restricted to officers, plus those troops who need some form of firearm but whose primary job means that carrying a full-length rifle is inconvenient—vehicle crews, cooks, headquarters staff, for example. In other services, such as the US forces, handgun ownership is far more widespread among regular troops, either through standardized distribution or through financed purchase by the soldiers themselves. But regardless of the levels of handgun ownership, it remains a backup weapon, with a fraction of the performance and capability of a rifle, submachine gun, or machine gun.

And yet, today's armed services still remain wedded to the idea of the handgun. There is something reassuring to a soldier to know that he has a weapon of last resort, should his main firearm jam up. In these days of complex war/peacekeeping operations, handguns can also be more socially acceptable in some instances. Rather than policing a generally peaceful

crowd with a threateningly visible machine gun, a handgun can remain discretely in its holster, ready for use but without the menace. Handguns can also be more practical for some roles, such as controlling prisoners within vehicles. So while the handgun is rather a poor relation to heavier small arms, it still has a place in the military small arms family, a place that Glock has successfully filled.

ABOVE: A Glock 17 with its 17-round polymer magazine. Often shooters will preserve the mag spring by only loading 14 or 15 rounds.

Special Forces and Regular Forces

As we saw earlier, the Glock was originally inspired by a military requirement, when Glock set out to design the gun from scratch for the Austrian Army. The reason he won that contract was not only that he fulfilled all the relevant specifications, but in many cases surpassed them. What the Austrian Army received was something revolutionary in terms of design, materials, and functionality, and it woke the military world to the next generation of handguns. Norway and Sweden soon followed in their acquisition of the Glock, and at the same time the gun was approved for NATO standardization.

However, the wheels of military procurement tend to turn slowly, so getting the Glock into major military purchasing programs would take time and persistence. Yet there was a market that was more immediately accessible within the military community, and that was special forces. Elite special forces units have a privileged status within the structure of a country's defense forces, and one of the perks that they often receive is the ability to purchase the best weapons on the market, rather than accept just the standard-issue arsenal of the wider military. Furthermore, special forces also require weaponry that the general soldiery don't need. For example, since the end of World War II, submachine guns have almost entirely been replaced by assault rifles, which have better capabilities all around. Special forces units, however, frequently rely upon submachine guns like the Heckler & Koch MP5, because these are actually better suited to close-range hostage-rescue missions, where overpenetration is to be avoided at all costs. Handguns are also absolutely relevant, both as back-up weapons in critical missions and also as concealed firepower.

Special Forces Users

If we look at a list of countries that presently use the Glock in military service, we find a high percentage of special forces users. Indeed, as soon as the Glock hit the market it seemed to appeal to elite soldiers. Early customers for the Glock 17 were police, state, and military forces such as the Venezuelan CAVIM Commandos, the Austrian Cobra Unit, German GSG9, and Syrian and Jordanian head-of-state guard. It is easy to see what appeals to special forces soldiers about the Glock. For example, if a unit was involved in VIP protection or under-cover work, heavy firepower in the form of submachine guns or rifles is often unacceptable from both a public relations point of view and from the concealability aspect. By having a Glock tucked away in a chest holster, however, the operator could draw on a 17-shot gun should trouble arise. The double-action mechanism was also appealing. During a hostage-rescue action, for example, a special forces soldier's worst nightmare is his primary weapon jamming during the confusion, flash-bangs, and violence of a close-quarters fight. Expert soldiers are therefore trained to transition out from the jammed gun to the handgun in a matter of seconds. The Glock was reassuring in this regard, as its lack of external safety switch meant that only a trigger pull was required to bring it to fire, but the internal safeties meant that there was little danger from an accidental discharge as the operator descended from helicopters, struggled through windows, and crossed obstacles.

Once the pistol was given the green light by elite users, it spread more easily out to the general military, aided by Glock's extremely efficient international marketing campaign. Hence today, the Glock serves globally with all manner and nationality of military units, just some of which are listed in the table here.

BELOW: Austrian *Jagdkommando* use Glock 17s as a primary handgun, although it is known as the P80 in their service.

COUNTRY	FORCE/UNIT
Austria	Austrian Armed Forces
Azerbaijan	Azerbaijan Special Military Services
Bangladesh	Bangladesh Army
Denmark	Slædepatruljen Sirius naval special forces
Finland	Defense Forces
India	National Security Guards, MARCOS, Para Commandos
Iraq	Iraq Security Forces
Israel	Israel Defense Forces
YAMAM	Shin Bet
Jordan	Royal Guard
Kosovo	Kosovo Security Force
Latvia	Latvian Military Forces
Lithuania	Lithuanian Armed Forces
Luxembourg	Luxembourg Army
Malaysia	Malaysian Armed Forces
Montenegro	Military of Montenegro
Netherlands	Armed Forces of the Netherlands
Norway	Norwegian Armed Forces
Pakistan	Pakistan Army
Poland	Military Gendarmerie
Portugal	Portuguese Marine Corps, Republican National Guard
Romania	Romanian Armed Forces
Russia	Ministry of Internal Affairs (MVD) special forces
Spain	Unidad Especial de Intervención (UEI) group of the Spanish Civil Guard
Sweden	Swedish Armed Forces
Switzerland	Swiss Armed Forces
United Kingdom	British Army
United States	1st Special Forces Operational Detachment-Delta, 75th Ranger Regiment
Uruguay	Uruguayan National Army
Venezuela	Venezuela Armed Forces
Yemen	Military of Yemen

Nor is military interest in the Glock waning. In fact, Glock continues to secure large new military contracts, and will doubtless continue to do so after this book is published. A good case in point has been the recent acquisition by the British Army.

The British Army and the Glock

In January 2013, a story broke in the British press about a new acquisition by the Ministry of Defense (MoD). They announced that after more than 70 years of relying upon the Browning Hi-Power as the standard-issue handgun, it was to be replaced by the G17 Gen4. Some 25,000 of the Glock handguns were to be purchased, at a cost of £9 million.

The shift was an important one for the British forces, and the press was right to take notice. The previous major firearms selection for the British armed services was the SA80 rifle, which replaced the redoubtable L1A1 self-loading rifle (the British variant of Fabrique Nationale de Herstal's global best-selling FN FAL) in 1985. That purchase was one of the most problematic in MoD history, the gun revealing some critical design flaws and chronic malfunctions in service. Only with a major series upgrade by Heckler & Koch, resulting in the SA80A2, did the rifle begin to inspire confidence in its handlers. So it was important that whatever new firearms the British forces invested in, they got the choice right.

During the era of the world wars, the British forces were equipped with several variants of Enfield or Webley revolvers, break-open types in .38 and .455 calibers. These were workmanlike guns, firearms that gave valiant service throughout two global conflicts, in theaters ranging from Western Europe to Burma. But by the end of World War II in 1945, they were truly beginning to show their age, especially against the new generations of semi-automatic pistols that were now on the scene.

So out went the Webleys and Enfields, and in came the Browning Hi-Power. It is worth exploring this weapon in a little more detail, so we can better judge why it was replaced in 2014. Despite the "Hi-Power" title, derived from the French *Grand Puissance*, the GP35 was actually no more powerful than any other 9mm (0.354in) handgun. However, it did break the mold in several important regards, and set a pattern that would have a direct influence on the future of gun design, including the Glock. Browning based the action on that of the Colt M1911, although Browning made some modifications to the trigger mechanism and used a shaped cam mechanism instead of a swinging link to control the slide and barrel engagement. It is a thoroughly reliable mechanism, hence it was appreciated by the military evaluators and performed well in trials.

The Hi-Power is a single-action gun. Thus, the hammer has to be cocked before the gun can be fired, either by manually operating the slide back and

ABOVE: Austrian *Jagdkommando* practice a high-risk detention, with one officer covering with his P80 (Glock 17).

forth, which loads a round in the chamber and cocks the hammer, or by pulling the hammer back with the thumb. Trigger pull alone cannot take the hammer through its cycle. What this meant tactically was that the best way to keep the gun at the ready but holstered was to have a round chambered, the hammer decocked and the external safety catch applied, to prevent an accidental discharge. All the soldier had to do to bring the weapon into action was to draw the gun, cock the hammer, take off the safety, and begin firing. One important point about the gun's operation, acknowledged in the official manual, was that dropping the gun onto a hard surface could result in an accidental discharge, even with the hammer in its dropped position. The real bonus of the Hi-Power at the time was its 13-round magazine, courtesy of a double-stack arrangement. Considering that the British forces had grown accustomed to just six rounds at the ready, 13 rounds was almost fantastical.

The Hi-Power was a quality gun, and it took its place within the arsenal of the British Army for more than 70 years. Even elite units such as the SAS took it as their sidearm, and carried it into action during engagements that included the 1980 Iranian Embassy Siege and the Falklands War.

Yet time passed, and eventually even the Hi-Power was beginning to show its age. With the end of the 1990s and the beginning of the 2000s, we see more signs of interest in replacing the weapon with something more modern. The catalyst for that change was the British involvement in the intensive conflicts in Iraq and Afghanistan. The Hi-Power went to war again, but because of the age of the stocks the Ministry of Defense had to source pistols urgently from elsewhere, while also looking into the future replacement. Furthermore, on a tactical level it was clear that the Hi-Power was outdated. The conflict in Afghanistan was very much based on British soldiers responding to endless series of ambushes, which often began with the detonation of an Improvised Explosive Device (IED) and ended just as abruptly. What mattered most of all in these situations was that the British troops could bring their weapons to bear as quickly as possible and lay down counter-fire to suppress the insurgents. Here the Hi-Power struggled.

RARE GLOCKS

Glocks are one of the world's most common handguns, but as well as extremely prolific models such as the G17 and the G19, there are several very rare Glocks. Elite units in particular have their own specific requirements for handguns, if only in terms of insignia and markings. One particularly rare Glock is the Glock P9M, pictured here. The P9M is essentially a G17, but built for the requirements of German counter-terrorist forces using the gun in watery environments. To ensure the reliability of the gun when wet, the magazine features drilled sides to allow for drainage, plus the gun's firing-pin spring was given extra power. The gun was also provided with a blue lanyard, to prevent the user losing the gun when dropped.

Like the G17 on which it is based, the P9M is a high-performing handgun, and was imported into Germany by SSME *Deutsche Waffen*. Other Glocks are rare mainly because of the markings on the slide. Being an internationally distributed gun, the Glock features a huge variety of national markings. The Austrian P80 (a military version of the G17, with some differences), for example, features an upside-down triangle in a circle on the slide and grip, to denote *Bundeswehr* service. More collectibly, there is even a series of Glock 19s that were issued to the Swiss Guard, who provide Papal protection. At the front end of the slide these guns actually feature the pontifical seal, a rare instance of religious iconography on an officially issued weapon.

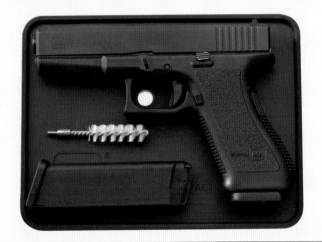

FACING PAGE: A Royal Marine presents the business end of his new G17 Gen4.

Whereas a Glock could literally be brought into action in a second—just pull it from the holster and start shooting—the Browning could take as long as four seconds to shoot, once the soldier had disengaged the safeties, according to defense insiders. Of course, the gun could be holstered with the safety off and the hammer back, but that was inviting a bullet in the leg.

The situation was clarified during another Parliamentary debate, this time in 2014 when the Secretary of States for Defense was Philip Dunne:

"Angus Robertson: To ask the Secretary of State for Defence how many Sig Sauer pistols his Department bought as an urgent operational requirement; and what the cost to the public purse was of that purchase.

Mr. Dunne: The cost to purchase a Sig Sauer [the P226] was less than that estimated for repairing unserviceable Brownings. To meet operational demands in Iraq and Afghanistan, between 2003 and 2013 6,600 Sig Sauer pistols and associated drop holsters were purchased to a total cost of around £2.5 million.

Purchases of the Sig Sauer pistol was an urgent operational order that was extant to the need to permanently replace the Browning. A full competition was carried out in 2012, and although seven different pistols, including the Sig Sauer, were considered and evaluated, the contract was awarded to replace the Browning with

BELOW: The G17 Gen4 was the ideal replacement for the British Browning Hi-Power, offering a substantial improvement in magazine capacity and ease of handling.

FACING PAGE: The Glock
19 has recently been
accepted into service
with the US Marine
Forces Special Operations
Command.

the Glock 17 pistol which performed overall best in both performance and cost."
(Hansard, February 2014)

Public details about the competition to which Dunne refers are few. What
we do know, however, is that the adoption of the Glock seems to be greeted
with general enthusiasm from within the ranks of the army. The MoD
announced the story thus, and commented on the trial:

*"The Glock 17 Gen 4 pistol is much lighter than the current Browning pistol,
and more accurate. It also has an increased magazine capacity of 17 9mm rounds,
compared to 13 rounds for the Browning.*

*Warrant Officer 1 Mark Anderson, Royal Marines, who trialed the Glock 17
before the contract was awarded, said: "Pistols are vital in close combat and are a
key part of a soldier's armory. Reliable, light and easy to carry, the Glock inspires
confidence and performs exceptionally well."*

*The MOD signed a £9m contract to provide the Armed Forces with more than
25,000 Glock sidearms including holsters.*

*Minister for Defence Equipment, Support, and Technology, Philip Dunne
said: "We are determined to provide our troops with the best possible personal kit
available and these new Glock 17s will give them greater firepower and accuracy
on operations."*

("Glock 17," http://www.army.mod.uk/equipment/23797.aspx)

The keyword in this quotation is "confidence." What Glock guns provide
to all users, whatever their profession or the levels of threat they face, is the
reassurance of a gun that can be brought into action quickly and fire when
the trigger is pulled.

The Glock's Future

We should not give the impression that the Glock was the only serious
contender in the UK competition. In fact, while the regular British Army
moved away to the Glock 17, the SAS and Special Boat Service (SBS)
shifted their loyalties to SIG. SIG handguns are worth deeper study here,
for they are one of the Glock's major competitors, with a list of military and
law-enforcement users to rival that of the Glock. Those who have adopted
Sigs include the US Navy SEALs, the Canadian Special Forces, the Finnish
Army, the Indian Army, Polish GROM, and Singapore Armed Forces, as

GLOCK 19 GEN4

DATE:
2010
CALIBER:
9 x 19 Safe Action
LENGTH:
7.28in (185mm)
BARREL LENGTH:
4.01in (102mm)
WEIGHT (LOADED):
30.18oz (855g)
**MAGAZINE CAPACITY
(STANDARD):**
15
EFFECTIVE RANGE:
50yds (45.72m)

well as dozens of specialist and regular law-enforcement agencies across the world. Note also that the SIG remains in service in the British Army, given that so many were acquired on an emergency basis. With the British forces the P226 is given the name L105A1 or, for an updated corrosion-resistant version, the L106A1. Another SIG in use is the P229, or in British terminology, the L117A2.

The main SIG models competing with the Glock are the P226, P228, and P229—we'll look at the P226 as the representative example, as the P228 and P229 are essentially more compact versions of the P226. The P226 was designed to be an entrant into the US armed forces' XM9 Service Pistol Trials during the 1980s, which were won by the Beretta 92, principally because the Beretta's costing package was better. The Glock and the SIG share the short-recoil operating system based on the Browning M1911 system, but like the Glock the SIG uses an enlarged breech section locking into the ejection port, rather than barrel lugs. (Note that this system was actually pioneered by SIG as far back as the 1930s; it was not a Glock invention.) The standards of machining are very high, with a stainless-steel slide and a hard anodized aluminum alloy frame. The construction makes the SIG very tough and resistant to corrosion. It also allows it to chamber not just the 9mm Parabellum, but also powerful .40 S&W and .357 SIG.

The SIG is a very user-friendly pistol and like the Glock it is designed to be both very safe and quick to bring into action. One of its defining features is a de-cocking lever, set on the left side of the frame above the magazine-release button. Being a hammer-actuated gun, when the SIG's side is pulled back and released, a round is loaded and the hammer is cocked ready to fire. Using the de-cocking lever, the operator can now drop the hammer safely

ABOVE: A Lithuanian
soldier serving with the
International Security
Assistance Force (ISAF)
in Afghanistan trains
with his Glock 17.

without connecting with the firing block pin, hence a round is not fired. In this mode, the gun is completely safe, even if knocked, hence it can be placed into a holster at the ready—the SIG has no external safety switch. Because the P226 is a double-action gun, all that it then takes to bring the gun into action is to draw it and pull the trigger.

The P226 series is extensive, just like the Glock. It comes in various formats, with features and versions including accessories rails, night sights, competition models, all-stainless-steel models, extended barrels, faster trigger reset types, and compact and subcompact versions. All told, the SIG package is extremely compelling, and competes head on with the Glock.

Rival Handguns

Nor is it the only gun putting up a fight against the march of the Glock. In 2005, Smith & Wesson, Glock's arch-rival within the United States, brought out its Military & Police (M&P) range of handguns, available in 9mm, .357 SIG, .40 S&W, and .45 ACP, and various barrel lengths. The M&P guns are striker-fired, Browning-type action handguns, with magazine capacities of up to 17 rounds, depending on the model. Crucially, the frame is now made of Zytol polymer, allied to a stainless steel slide and barrel. The guns also have ambidextrous slide stops, loaded chamber indicators, and integral Picatinny rails at the front of the frame for tactical accessories. There is no external safety switch, but instead the gun has a host of internal safeties. Because of its double-action-only (DAO) trigger system, the M&P can, like the Glock, be drawn and fired immediately, using trigger-pull alone.

BELOW: The SIG P226 is one of the Glock's principal rivals, the gun delivering the same kind of functionality, reliability, and power.

The list of contenders to the Glock throne go on and on, with excellent new weapons now being manufactured by the likes of Beretta, Ruger, Fabrique Nationale, and Heckler & Koch. This is a round-about way of saying that while Glock has grown dominant in certain markets, and sales continue to grow, the company must never rest on its laurels. Other companies are innovating continually, and so must Glock if it is to maintain the reputation it has fought so hard and fast to secure.

U.S. Army Contract

Another moment of import for the Glock will be the eventual replacement, in the US armed services, of the Beretta M9 (the militarized Beretta 92). From the early 2000s onward, the US military has been engaged in discussions and experiments concerning its next-generation of small arms, including replacements for the Beretta. The first serious steps were taken in

2004 with the Future Handgun System (FHS) program, which began looking at commercial pistol products that could serve as possible alternatives to the Beretta within the US Army and other services. At the same time, the US Special Operations Command (USSOCOM) also began a similar program, known as the Special Operations Forces Combat Pistol (SOFCS). In 2005 these two programs were merged into the Joint Combat Pistol (JCP) program, although it was still run by USSOCOM. Specifications given in the new program made it clear what type of handgun was required—"A caliber .45 pistol, two [2] standard-capacity magazines, operator's manual, and cleaning kit," some with internal-only safeties, and some with external safety switches. Some key points are reproduced here:

1.1. Performance Requirements.

1.1.1. Reliability. The JCP shall have a Mean Rounds Between Stoppage (MRBS) of 2000 rounds (T) and 5000 rounds (O) firing A475 and A483 ammunition. The JCP shall have a Mean Rounds Between Failure (MRBF) of 5000 rounds (T) and 10,000 rounds (O) firing A475 and A483 ammunition. The weapon shall function reliably when operated in extreme environments per section 3.6.

1.1.2. Accuracy. When fired from a rest, at a range of 50 meters, the mean radius of a 10-shot group fired from the JCP shall not be greater than A) 3.15 inches or B)1.8 inches over baseline ammunition performance, whichever is less (T). Baseline ammunition performance is defined as the average mean radius plus two sample standard deviations of three 10-shot groups fired from a test barrel at 50m.

1.1.3. Service Life. The JCP shall have a service life of 20,000 rounds (T), greater than 20,000 (O), using A475 .45 ACP Ball, and/or A483 .45 ACP match ammunition. The JCP should be capable of

BELOW: The Smith & Wesson M&P pistol is, like the Glock, a polymer frame gun with a striker-fired, double-action mechanism.

ABOVE: US Navy personnel participate in their Beretta M9 qualification course on board USS *Laboon*.

a service life of 20,000 rounds when firing 5% AA18 .45 +P ammunition (O). Receiver service life shall be defined as a receiver that is at the end of its usable life cycle.

1.2. Physical description.

1.2.1. Magazine Capacity. The JCP shall have a standard magazine capacity of no less than eight [8] rounds (T), greater than eight [8] rounds (O) of .45 ACP ammunition. The JCP shall also have a high-capacity magazine of no less than ten [10] rounds (T), fifteen [15] rounds (O), of .45 ACP ammunition.

1.2.2. Pistol Lanyard Attachment Point. The JCP shall have a rigid attachment point for a lanyard (T). The JCP lanyard attachment point shall not interfere with the JCP control features or magazine unloading and reloading, and shall minimize snag hazard (T).

1.2.3. Accessory Rail. The JCP shall have an integral MIL-STD-1913 rail for the attachment of accessories (T). The rail shall be located forward of the trigger guard on the lower portion of the frame (T).

ABOVE: A US Special
Forces soldier delivers
fire from a G19. Unlike
the regular US Army, the
Special Forces community
has tended to gravitate
towards Glocks and SIGs.

1.2.4. Surface Finish. The JCP surface finish shall be non-reflective, resistant to peeling, flaking, and chipping, and require a minimum of operator preventive maintenance (T). Internal coatings should be lubricious/low friction mitigating the use of lubricants (O). Non-metallic components shall be fungus and battlefield chemical resistant (T). JCP materials and coatings shall protect the pistol from degradation in all climates and geographical areas including maritime, coastal, desert, tropical jungle, arctic, urban areas, and mountain environments (T). The materials and coatings shall minimize the attraction of dust and contamination (T).

1.3. Weapon controls.

1.3.1. Action: The JCP shall function in double-action/single-action (DA/SA) or double-action only (DAO) including Striker-Fired Action (SFA) (T). The JCP should have a modular action mechanism that allows reconfiguration at the unit level without modification to the weapon's major assemblies (O).

1.3.2. Trigger Pull: All DA/SA pistols shall have a consistent trigger pull of eight to ten [8-10] pounds on Double Action, and a consistent trigger pull of four to six [4-6] pounds on Single Action and all DAO pistols shall have a trigger pull of five to eight [5-8] pounds (T). All pistols shall have a trigger pull that is consistent within one [1] pound from average pull (T). When pressure is applied to the JCP trigger and then released, the trigger shall reset to its forward-most position, even if the pistol is not fired (T). The operator shall be capable of pulling the trigger, without shifting the firing grip as will be tested in section 3.6.3.

1.3.3. Magazine Release/Tactical Reload: The JCP shall allow the magazine, empty or with any number of rounds loaded, to drop free of the magazine well when the magazine release is activated (T). The magazine shall fall free when the pistol grip is held at any angle from 0 degrees vertical (normal firing attitude) to 45 degrees from vertical (T). The magazine shall also be capable of manual extraction when held at any other angle (T). The pistol shall be capable of firing with a chambered round and

BELOW: A Glock representative explains features of the G37 Gen4 .45-cal pistol at the 35th annual SHOT Show, 2013, in Las Vegas.

without a magazine in the magazine well (T). The pistol shall reliably fire when the pistol has a round in the chamber and a fully loaded magazine is inserted with the slide fully forward and the pistol is fired (T). The operator shall be capable of operating the magazine release with the firing hand (T). The operator should be capable of operating the magazine release without shifting the firing grip (O).

1.3.4. Ergonomic Enhancements: The JCP shall be operable for a range of operators from the 5th to 95th percentile per section 3.6.3. To aid in this, the JCP should incorporate a modular grip adjustment system to provide enhanced ergonomics (O).

Sights: The JCP sights shall provide rapid target acquisition and shall be optimized for snag-resistant rapid deployment (T). The JCP sights shall be replaceable at the organizational level (T). The JCP sights shall be drift-adjustable for windage (T). The JCP sights shall be self-illuminating for low light situations without ambient or external light source "charging" (T).

Looking through this list of requirements, it is evident how much Glock was well positioned to compete for this prize. At every level—mag capacity, controls, resistance to wear, accuracy, caliber and performance, ergonomic layout—it was fulfilling the criteria of the competition already in its range of guns. Back in the 1980s, Glock had resisted the temptation to enter the US Army's pistol competition, but this time around it submitted the Glock 21SF, offering the power of the .45-caliber round allied to shorter-frame dimensions, so it could be handled by the entire cross-section of armed forces personnel. Other guns in the running were:

- Heckler & Koch HK45C
- SIG P220 Combat
- Ruger P345
- Smith & Wesson M&P
- Beretta PX4 Storm
- Taurus PT 24/7 OSS
- Fabrique Nationale FNP45-USG
- HS-45 (Springfield Armory XD)
- Para-Ordnance LDA 1911

Replacing any gun in a large military force is always a partly political decision, and in the United States the decision was fraught with interest groups and legal agendas. While few would deny that something needed to change, the way it was to be changed was the subject of hot debate. Some preferred a simple Beretta upgrade; others wanted a replacement pistol but from a US manufacturer; others leaned toward modern European guns such as the Glock or SIG. Inertia built up, and in 2006 the JCP program was indefinitely postponed. The Beretta M9 remained in service.

But this is not the end of the story. In 2013, the hunt for a new US military handgun began again. By this time, the requirement was more pressing. Like the British, the United States had by this point in time gained the hard experience of more than a decade of combat in Iraq and Afghanistan. The M9s that had been in the inventory for many years were

ABOVE: **US soldiers with the 1st Battalion, 10th Special Forces Group (Airborne), Detachment Alpha 0114, train their Hungarian counterparts in handling the G19.**

starting to show mechanical problems, plus many soldiers felt that they lagged behind more modern pistols in terms of functionality. Therefore, the US army issued a Request for Information (RFI), to gather feedback from the firearms industry about the types of guns that could be offered. The new program was called the Modular Handgun System (MHP), and the RFI ran as follows:

As of 11 March 2013, Response Date has been modified FROM: 11 March 2013 TO: 29 March 2013.

The Program Manager for Soldier Weapons (PM SW) Picatinny Arsenal, NJ 07860-5000, on behalf of the Program Executive Office Soldier, Fort Belvoir, VA 22060-5422, is assessing handgun technologies as well as production capacity of the US small arms industrial base. This announcement constitutes an official Request for Information (RFI).

BELOW: A US Navy officer armed with a Glock participates in a small-arms course aboard a Hellenic navy training ship. Note how the other participants have blue-framed training Glocks.

To facilitate the assessment, the following information is requested:

1. Performance Improvement: Request information on potential improvements in handgun performance in the areas of accuracy and dispersion out to 50m, terminal performance, modularity, reliability, and durability in all environments.

• The handgun and ammunition combination should, at a range of 50 meters, have a 90% or better probability of hit on a 4 inch circle when fired from a test fixture. It must maintain this throughout the life of the system. Systems are encouraged to utilize ergonomic and design improvements to minimize the effects of greater recoil energies, reducing the degradation of shooter-in-the-loop dispersion thereby improving the probability of hit.

• Modularity includes but is not limited to compatibility with accessory items to include tactical lights, lasers, and sound suppressors. There is specific interest in designs that would be adaptable and/or adjustable to provide enhanced ergonomics that ensure 5th percentile female through 95th percentile male military personnel access to controls, such as the safety, magazine release, slide release, and all other applicable controls. There is also interest in designs that offer these enhanced ergonomics while providing full ambidextrous controls.

• The handgun ammunition's terminal ballistics will be evaluated at ranges of 0–50m, over 0–14 inches of ballistic gelatin, to determine whether it provides more lethality when compared to the current U.S. Military M882 ammunition fired from the M9. Ammunition evaluated will meet international law of war conventions that bound current general purpose military ammunition. The Pistol evaluated must be capable of chamber pressures equal to or greater than SAAMI specification for the given cartridge, with prolonged reliability equal to or greater than the current M9. However, the ability to accommodate higher chamber pressures in excess of 20% over SAAMI spec without degradation of reliability is of specific interest.

• Reliability and Durability includes but is not limited to Mean Rounds

ABOVE: **An Iraqi police recruit engages a target with his G17 following training by US and Iraqi Army personnel.**

between Stoppage (MRBS), Mean Rounds Between Failure (MRBF), and Service Life. There is specific interest in designs with ratings of at least 2,000 rounds MRBS, 10,000 rounds MRBF, and 35,000 round Service Life.

2. Production capacity estimates. Request information on minimum and maximum monthly production rates for a military handgun and associated ammunition as well as the lead times to achieve these production rates. This estimate should consider a US-based production facility by the third year of deliveries. This capacity should be above and beyond any current production orders or current sales. If new facilities are planned or required, so state. A list of State and Federal agencies, as well as foreign governments, that have adopted the handgun should also be included.

3. Detailed descriptions of proposed handguns to include pictures, brochures, etc. that will convey the principles as well as general and specific capabilities behind the submissions. Physical dimensions, weight, and safety features should be included.

4. Summarized and detailed test data from any certified test facility that addresses improvements in the areas proposed. Test operating procedures utilized and independent evaluations are also solicited.

5. Rough Order of Magnitude (ROM) Estimate. Request estimated pricing for the submission based on the following quantities: 250,000 to 550,000 handguns.

(Department of the Army, Army Contracting Command)

As with the JHP competition, the general specifications are entirely suited to the Glock range. The Gen4 standard of the Glock is especially fitting for the modularity criterion, giving the user not only the ability to install a variety of tactical fittings, but also to adjust to a certain extent the ergonomics of the grip. The accuracy and power demands are also within the scope of the Glock.

At the time of writing, the MHP is just about to enter its testing phase. Given what has happened to previous programs, the outcome is uncertain, but the popular press is replete with authorities calling for the serious consideration of the Glock. Future readers of this book are likely to know the outcome, but suffice to say that this could be the moment when the Glock takes the biggest slice of the global military market.

Looking back, we have to remain impressed by the fact that Gaston Glock, a man with no previous experience of developing firearms, managed to become one of the world's leading firearms manufacturers and distributors in a little over a decade. The G17 established the benchmark of innovation, and the subsequent models took that innovation onward. As Gaston Glock moves on through his 80s, it will be up to new generations of Glock engineers and designers to ensure that the trend for cutting-edge firearms continues into the future.

BELOW: Paramilitary soldiers of the Kosovan Army, who wear the G17 as the standard sidearm.

Further Reading

Anderson, J., and Vale Van Atta. "Qaddafi Buying Austrian Plastic Pistols," *Washington Post* (Jan 15, 1985).

Barrett, Paul M. Glock: *The Rise of America's Gun* (New York: Broadway Books, 2013).

California Highway Patrol. *Test and Evaluation: 10mm Semi-Automatic Pistol* (May 1990).

FBI Training Division. "Executive Summary of Justification for Law Enforcement Partners" (Quantico, VA, FBI Academy, May 6, 2014).

House of Representatives Committee on the Judiciary Subcommittee on Crime, "Firearms that Can Escape Detection" (1986).

Kasler, Peter Alan. *Glock: The New Wave in Combat Handguns* (Boulder, CO: Paladin Press, 1992).

Kokalis, Peter. *"Plastic Perfection," Soldier of Fortune* (October 1984).

McNab, Chris. *Deadly Force: Firearms and American Law Enforcement, from the Wild West to the Streets of Today* (General Military, 2009).

Sweeney, Patrick. *Glock Deconstructed* (Iola, WI: Gun Digest Books, 2013).

Sweeney, Patrick. *The Gun Digest Book of the Glock,* 2nd edition (Iola, WI: Gun Digest Books, 2008).

Glock Regional Headquarters—Contact Details

EUROPE

GLOCK Ges.m.b.H., P.O. Box 9, A-2232 Deutsch Wagram, Austria

Tel.: +43 (0) 2247-90300-0 Fax: +43 (0) 2247-90300-312

UNITED STATES

GLOCK, Inc., 6000 Highlands Parkway, Smyrna, GA 30082 United States

Tel.: +1 770-432 1202 Fax: +1 770-433 8719

SOUTH AMERICA

GLOCK America S.A., Plaza Independencia 831, Office 802, 11100 Montevideo Uruguay

Tel.: +598 - 2-902 2227 Fax: +598 - 2-902 2230

GLOCK ASIA-PACIFIC

GLOCK Asia Pacific Limited, Unit 3, LG/F, OB1, 92 Siena Avenue, DB North Plaza, Discovery Bay, Lantau, N.T., Hong Kong

Tel.: +852 2375-3858 Fax: +852 2654-7089

MIDDLE EAST

GLOCK Middle East FZE, P.O. Box 54260, Dubai, United Arab Emirates

Tel.: +971 - 4-299 5779 Fax: +971 - 4-299 4442

Glossary

Battery: A gun is 'in battery' when a cartridge is seated fully in the chamber and the component parts of the gun are properly configured for firing.

Blowback: A system of firearms operation in which the power for extraction and ejection comes from the recoil imparted on the empty cartridge case.

Bore: The interior of a gun barrel.

Breech: The rear end of the barrel or bore.

Chamber: The rear section of the barrel in which cartridges are seated for firing.

Disconnector: A mechanical device that prevents the weapon firing repeatedly when the trigger is held down.

Double action: A handgun mechanism in which trigger pull alone both cocks and releases the hammer/striker.

Extractor: The part of the gun responsible for removing spent cartridge cases from the chamber.

Magazine: A container inserted into or integral with a firearm, responsible for holding and feeding ammunition.

Rifling: Helical grooves cut into a bore to impart stabilizing gyroscopic spin to a bullet.

Sear: A part of the trigger group that holds the hammer, striker or bolt back under pressure. When the trigger is pulled, the sear is mechanically disconnected from the firing mechanism, allowing the firing mechanism to be released to strike the primer.

Short recoil: A system of firearms operation in which the barrel and bolt/slide are locked together for a short distance (shorter than the length of the cartridge) during recoil, before unlocking to allow the bolt/slide to go through the full recoil cycle.

Single action: A handgun mechanism in which a hammer or striker has to be cocked manually before it can be released by the trigger.

Slide: In handguns, the moving upper section of the gun which facilitates, under the firing impulse, the actions of loading, extraction and ejection.

Suppressor: A fitting attached to a gun at the muzzle, designed to contain and slow the propellant gases and thereby reduce the gun's firing sound.

Windage: 1) The side-to-side adjustment of a gun sight; 2) Making an aiming allowance for the effects of wind direction and speed.

Glock Handguns by Caliber

Below are the guns listed on the Glock website at the time of writing, arranged by caliber:

CALIBER	TYPE	MODEL
9 x 19mm	Standard	G17
		G17 Gen4
	Compact	G19
		G19 Gen4
	Subcompact	G26
		G26 Gen4
.40	Standard	G22
		G22 Gen4
	Compact	G23
		G23 Gen4
	Subcompact	G27
		G27 Gen4
10mm Auto	Standard	G20
		G20 Gen4
		G20 SF
	Subcompact	G29
		G29 Gen4
		G29 SF
	Long Slide	G40 Gen4 MOS

CALIBER	TYPE	MODEL
.45 Auto	Standard	G21
		G21 Gen4
		G21 SF
	Subcompact	G30
		G30 Gen4
		G30 SF
		G30S
	Subcompact slimline	G36
.45 GAP	Standard	G37
		G37 Gen4
	Compact	G38
	Subcompact	G39
.380 Auto	Compact	G25
	Subcompact	G28
	Subcompact slimline	G42
.357	Standard	G31
		G31 Gen4
	Compact	G32
		G32 Gen4
	Subcompact	G33
		G33 Gen4
Training and practice	Cutaway	Gen3 – G17, G19, G20, G21, G22, G23
		Gen4 – G17
	Practice	G22P
	Reset	G17R

CALIBER CONVERSIONS		
.22	–	5.7mm
.25 ACP	–	6.4mm
7.62mm	–	.295in
.32 ACP	–	7.8mm
9mm Parabellum	–	.354in
.380 Auto	–	9mm
.357 Magnum	–	9.1mm
.40 S&W	–	10.2mm
10mm Auto	–	.40in
.44 Magnum	–	10.9mm
.45 ACP	–	11.5mm
.45 GAP	–	11.5mm

LEFT: The main calibers used in this book are listed with their conventional metric and imperial conversions.

OPPOSITE: Here is a complete list of the Glock range of handguns in numbered order, with main specifications included.

MODEL NUMBER	CARTRIDGE	TOTAL LENGTH (MM)	(IN)	BARREL LENGTH (MM)	(IN)	MAGAZINE CAPACITY STANDARD	OPTIONAL
17, 17C	9×19mm	204	8.03	114	4.48	17	10, 33
17L	9×19mm	225	8.86	153	6.02	17	10, 33
17 Gen4	9×19mm	202	7.95	114	4.48	17	10, 33
18, 18C	9×19mm	186	7.32	116	4.57	33	10, 17, 19, 31
19, 19C	9×19mm	187	7.36	102	4.01	15	10, 17, 33
19 Gen4	9×19mm	185	7.28	102	4.01	15	10, 17, 33
20, 20C	10 mm Auto	209	8.22	117	4.60	15	10
20 Gen4, 20 SF	10 mm Auto	204	8.03	117	4.60	15	10
21, 21C	.45 ACP	209	8.22	117	4.60	13	10
21 Gen4, 21 SF	.45 ACP	204	8.03	117	4.60	13	10
22, 22C	.40 S&W	204	8.03	114	4.48	15	10, 22
22 Gen4	.40 S&W	202	7.95	114	4.48	15	10, 22
23, 23C	.40 S&W	187	7.36	102	4.01	13	10, 15, 22
23 Gen4	.40 S&W	185	7.28	102	4.01	13	10, 15, 22
24, 24C	.40 S&W	225	8.86	153	6.02	15	10, 17, 22, 24
25	.380 ACP	187	7.36	102	4.01	15	–
26	9×19mm	165	6.49	87	3.42	10	15, 17, 33
26 Gen4	9×19mm	163	6.41	87	3.42	10	15, 17, 33
27	.40 S&W	165	6.49	87	3.42	9	13, 15, 22
27 Gen4	.40 S&W	163	6.41	87	3.42	9	13, 15, 22
28	.380 ACP	165	6.49	87	3.42	10	–
29	10mm Auto	177	6.96	96	3.77	10	15
29 Gen4, 29 SF	10mm Auto	175	6.88	96	3.77	10	15
30, 30S	.45 ACP	177	6.96	96	3.77	10	13
30 Gen4, 30 SF	.45 ACP	175	6.88	96	3.77	10	13
31, 31C	.357	204	8.03	114	4.48	15	10
31 Gen4	.357	202	7.95	114	4.48	15	10
32, 32C	.357	187	7.36	102	4.01	13	10, 15
32 Gen4	.357	185	7.28	102	4.01	13	10, 15
33	.357	165	6.49	87	3.42	9	13, 15
33 Gen4	.357	163	6.41	87	3.42	9	13, 15
34	9×19mm	224	8.81	135	5.31	17	10, 33
34 Gen4	9×19mm	222	8.74	135	5.31	17	10, 33
35	.40 S&W	224	8.81	135	5.31	15	10, 22
35 Gen4	.40 S&W	222	8.74	135	5.31	15	10, 22
36	.45 ACP	177	6.96	96	3.77	6	–
37	.45 GAP	204	8.03	114	4.48	10	–
37 Gen4	.45 GAP	202	7.95	114	4.48	10	–
38	.45 GAP	187	7.36	102	4.01	8	10
39	.45 GAP	165	6.49	87	3.42	6	8, 10
40 Gen4	10mm Auto	241	9.49	153	6.02	15	–
41 Gen4	.45 ACP	226	8.90	135	5.31	13	10
42	.380 ACP	151	5.94	83	3.25	6	–

Index

Numbers in **bold** indicate
illustrations and photographs.

Picture Credits

Alamy: 6 (Peter Titmuss), 8 (Jack Sullivan), 29 (AF Archive), 32 (DPA), 40 (Zuma Press), 41 (Radharc Images), 45 (F4Foto), 46 (Zuma Press), 48 (AF Archive), 56 (Thomas Goodwin), 59 (Zuma Press), 60/61 (Jeremy Gassman), 72 (Stephen Barnes), 76 (Gerry Rousseau), 90 (AF Archive), 96 (Prettyphoto), 113 (Mikael Karlsson), 114/115 (Zuma Press), 122 (Arthur Turner), 144 (David L. Moore), 153 (Stephen Barnes), 163 (Findlay), 164 (Michael Karlsson), 169 (Zuma Press), 172 (Joeysworld.com), 174 (Michael Karlsson), 176 (Tim Graham), 179 (Michael Matthews), 186/187 (Zuma Press), 189 (SC Photos), 205 (Andrew Chittock), 206 (Sandy O'Neal), 215 (Kasia Nowak)

AKG Images/Interfoto: 77, 117 top, 199

Art-Tech: 17, 18, 43, 52

Austrian Armed Forces: 34, 195, 198

Cody Images: 14, 15, 204

Colourblue: 118 bottom, 119-121 all, 123-125 all, 133-138 all, 141-142 all, 145-149 all

Corbis: 25 (Jacques Langevin), 39 (Jacques Langevin), 42 (Anthony Anex), 101 (Snakeman), 150 (Stephanie Kuykendal), 154 (Jacques Langevin), 155 (Russell Boyce), 160 (Zohra Bensemra), 165 (Tetra), 173 (Ralph D. Freso)

Depositphotos: 30 (Pinkblue), 73 (Keviuk), 104 (Kataklinger), 180/181 (ctppix)

Dreamstime: 12 (Andriy Baranovskiy), 62 (Kajornyot)

Federal Bureau of Investigation: 84 bottom

Getty Images: 37 (Stephen Morton), 49 (Stephen Morton), 50 (Yuttana Udomdangaram), 55 (Mario Villafuerte), 64 (MCT), 83 (Fred Dufour), 128 (Joe Amon), 139 (Washington Post), 156 (Steve Russell), 158 (Scott Olson), 161 (Jay Directo), 167 (David McNew), 184 (Mail Today), 192 (Bay Ismoyo), 194 (Jo Raedle)

Ken Lunde: 118 top

Press Association: 23 (John Stillwell), 36 (David Goldman), 89 (Mike Groll), 112 (Doug Strickland/Chattanooga Times Free Press Nooga.com), 201 (John Stillwell), 209 (Julie Jacobson)

Rex Features: 7 (APA), 200 (Andrew Linnett/MoD)

Royal Canadian Mounted Police: 10

TopFoto: 100 (David Lassman)

US Department of Defense: 13, 28, 31, 51, 71, 129, 159, 190, 207, 208, 211, 212, 214

All other images courtesy of **Glock, Inc.**